Hatfield House

THE FIRST 400 YEARS

Darling Laurie
With much love
Han x

Hatfield House

THE FIRST 400 YEARS

Edited by Hannah Salisbury

First published in 2011 by Gascoyne Holdings Press
Hatfield House, Hatfield, Hertfordshire AL9 5NQ

Produced by Dovecote Press Ltd
Stanbridge, Wimborne Minster, Dorset BH21 4JJD

ISBN 978-0-9568579-1-0

Designed by Humphrey Stone
Printed and bound in Italy by L.E.G.O.

All papers used by The Dovecote Press are natural,
recyclable products made from wood grown in sustainable,
well-managed forests

A CIP catalogue record for this book is available
from the British Library

Contents

Foreword

HANNAH SALISBURY

A FOUR HUNDREDTH ANNIVERSARY provides a good reason to boast. From the first time I came to Hatfield, I was intrigued to read about previous incumbents of the House, what they did and how they lived. It may seem peculiar, but I find it fascinating to know that John Tradescant bought two garden rakes and two pairs of shears in April 1612 and that the Four Seasons tapestries were laid out on the South Front and brushed to remove the moth eggs in the 1920s. I hope that future generations will be equally amused by the fact that my husband still keeps a domestic chaplain for daily morning prayers, and that it cost £30 to replace a trio of Silkie bantams killed by an urban fox. The hours I spent foraging amongst the papers stored in the Muniment Room, under the patient and ever-knowledgable Robin Harcourt Williams, made me want to record something of our time here for future generations to enjoy.

An excellent way to produce a book is to get 16 contributors to write it for you. My co-authors have been incredibly generous with their time and expertise, and describe the many subjects of the Estate today from wonderfully different perspectives – from a retired mechanic and an arable foreman to academics and present custodians.

The story of Hatfield House unsurprisingly starts with its building, and like a thread through the book, its maintenance, rebuilding and evolution crop up time and again. But an Estate such as Hatfield is so much more than just a house: by looking at the chapter headings one realises the extraordinary breadth of skill and number of enterprises needed to run such a place. We are fortunate in having a young team to manage these projects. Such a white elephant as Hatfield House needs more than just glue to hold it together: it thrives on constant care, fresh ideas, and the vigour which comes with every new generation.

Hatfield House has a role to play – as it always has had – and I feel fortunate to have been given a part. It is very good fun to have a husband with energy, taste and vision, and with luck, what he achieves in this generation will ensure the future of this great place.

Our great friend Douglas Slater, whose idea this book was, and who has contributed two chapters, suggested that this should be a book to dip into. I hope you enjoy doing exactly that.

Hannah Salisbury

KEY TO PLAN OF HATFIELD PARK

1. Georges Gate
2. Car and Coach park
3. Bloody Hollow Adventure Playground
4. Hatfield Park Farm
5. Church Hall
6. St Etheldreda's Church
7. Salisbury Chapel and tombs
8. Fore St Lodge
9. Hatfield Real Tennis Club
10. The Old Palace
11. Old Palace Garden
12. West Garden Entrance
13. Sundial Garden
14. Moore at Hatfield exhibition
15. Shrubbery
16. Viewing Bay
17. South Front
18. North Front
19. East Garden Entrance
20. East Garden Maze
21. Restaurant
22. Riding School Conference Centre
23. Stable Yard Shopping
24. Home Yard
25. Melon Ground
26. Carters Row
27. Station Lodge – to rail station
28. To Vineyard
29. To Queen Elizabeth Oak Showground
30. New Pond

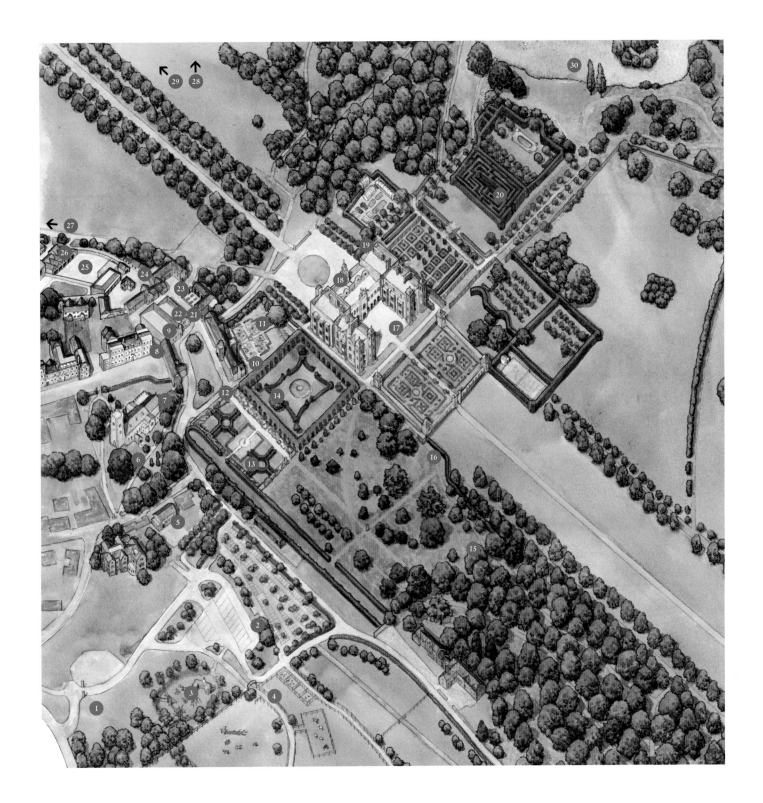

Hatfield: the last 400 years and taking guard for the next 400

ROBERT SALISBURY

AT THE TOP of the elaborate central doorway of the South Front of Hatfield House, are carved the figures 1611. These figures represent the date by which the House was finished. In reality, the carved date embodies more an aspiration than an accomplished fact, for there remained much to do. Some argue that this has remained the case ever since. Nevertheless, no other date can stake a better claim to mark the House's completion, so we have taken the building itself as our guide and determined to celebrate our four hundredth anniversary this year.

What is it that we are celebrating? Well, there is always a great deal to be said for throwing a party, particularly at a time of economic gloom and in an age dominated by a destructively self-righteous and hypocritical commentariat. Equally, that the House has survived, and in the care of the family that built it, is something to celebrate in itself.

1. SURVIVAL – THE LAST 400 YEARS

That it has survived is more a matter of luck than good management. One wing was gutted by fire in 1835, along with the Dowager of the day, and the rest of the House was only saved by what seemed, to the early Victorians, divine intervention. Indeed, the threat of fire is a

OPPOSITE *The Clock Tower, 1611, from the South Front.*

constant. We had a narrow squeak in 1988 in the clock tower, and it was surely a miracle that Prime Minister Salisbury's electric wires did not start a conflagration when he installed electric light in 1881. As dangerous to the House's survival, and to their own, were a depressingly high proportion of the Salisburys themselves. It is true that a number of them were distinguished servants of the Crown, but, particularly in the second half of the seventeenth century and for most of the eighteenth, far too many were as feckless and incompetent as they were stupid. They squandered a great inheritance and, by the middle of the eighteenth century, were so strapped for cash that the Salisbury of the day had to abandon Hatfield for a smaller establishment near Baldock. There he lived surrounded by a rapacious mistress and a brood of illegitimate children. That Hatfield survived his incumbency is largely thanks to the loyalty and good sense of his wife, Elizabeth Keate, who kept the show on the road and enabled her son to enter into some sort of inheritance.

Indeed, this was not the last time that our branch of the Cecil family was saved by a strong-minded wife. Miss Fanny Gascoyne married James, 2nd Marquess of Salisbury in 1821, bringing with her a great fortune and the respectful admiration of the 1st Duke of Wellington (who was never immune to hero-worship, especially from personable young women). Her fortune helped pay off her mother-in-law's gambling debts and repaired, at least to a degree, the financial depredations of seven generations of her husband's ancestors. Her gentle charm smoothed over her husband's rougher edges. Her mother-in-law was the Dowager who perished in the 1835 fire. An Irish hoyden from Hillsborough Castle, she was much lampooned by the wits and cartoonists of the day as 'Old Sarum', but she did much to bring the family back into the great world and to rekindle its interest in politics.

The other nineteenth century Lady Salisbury without whom the family could not have flourished was Georgina Alderson, wife of the Salisbury who was three times Prime Minister under Queen Victoria. Formidable, intel-

Lady Emily Mary Hill, 1st Marchioness of Salisbury, 1750–1835, by Sir Joshua Reynolds.

Frances Mary, 2nd Marchioness of Salisbury, 1800–1839, (born Fanny Gascoyne, the Gascoyne heiress), by Sir Thomas Lawrence.

Mildred, Lady Burghley (died 1589), mother of Robert Cecil, a painting attributed to Hans Eworth.

ligent, domineering, unconventional and uncaring of appearances, she was as devoted to her husband as he was to her. She helped him overcome his shyness and nerves and became an indispensable partner in his political life, providing a stable and happy, if unconventional, family for her intellectual, pessimistic and paradoxical husband.

In fact, strong-minded women run like a thread through the family's history and, if pressed to identify one reason for our intermittent influence in the world of politics and, especially, our continuing survival, our ability to marry formidable wives is by far the most convincing explanation. It is a knack that the great Lord Burghley himself twice demonstrated in the sixteenth century, as had his father, once. Robert Cecil, the builder of the House, mourned his own wife's early death until his own excruciating end in 1612. It is perhaps superfluous to note that the knack has not been lost in the twentieth century.

These formidable women, with one exception, differ substantially from the wives of other British noble families. Most of the latter were either aristocratic or heiresses, or both. In our case, only Fanny Gascoyne was an heiress and she was certainly not aristocratic. Burghley himself was the archetypal new man, perhaps the most outstanding example of the new middle class which rose to prominence under the Tudors. His wives were no more aristocratic than he was and, like many arrivistes, he tried hard to prove he was of nobler descent than his contemptuous contemporaries allowed. He took excessive pleasure in his daughter's disastrous marriage to the impeccably high-born Lord Oxford. Of the other Salisbury wives, apart from the incinerated Lady Emily Mary Hill of Hillsborough, the most formidable until the twentieth century were wholly middle-class. Elizabeth Keate was the daughter of the rector of Hatfield; Fanny Gascoyne was the grand-daughter of a Liverpool speculator who had served the Earls of Derby and of a Lord Mayor of London; while Georgina Alderson was the daughter of a judge, whose lack of social standing so attracted the disapproval of her father-in-law (Fanny Gascoyne's husband!) that he cut off his second son for marrying her – a disgraceful example of snobbery corrupting judgement.

How paradoxical it is that the family that produced

Georgina, 3rd Marchioness of Salisbury, 1827–1899, by George Richmond.

3rd Marquess of Salisbury, 1830–1903, wearing the black and gold robes of Chancellor of the University of Oxford, by George Richmond.

Prime Minister Salisbury, often thought to be the last example in this country of aristocratic government, should in fact turn out to be essentially middle class.

It is a splendid instance of the British capacity to adapt and to absorb new men of ability and fortune. It is a capacity that the ancient regimes of continental Europe did not have, with fatal consequences both for their constitutions and their ruling elites. I cannot help but speculate as to whether the British in the twenty-first century will be able to evolve to meet the demands of today and to flourish, or whether our sons will look back on the bureaucracy of our post-imperial twilight much as we contemplate the pre-1914 Austro-Hungarian Empire.

2. SURVIVAL – THE NEXT 400 YEARS

In its own way, Hatfield House will also have to adapt if it is to survive and flourish. The family are still its custodians and can make choices in planning for its future – and, indeed, in planning for its own future as a family. Our freedom of action is circumscribed by legislation, taxation, regulation, bureaucracy, the European Union and all the other deposits that befur the arteries of today's British state.

In coming to make those choices, our four hundredth anniversary provides us not only with an opportunity to celebrate our history and to thank God for our luck in surviving the vicissitudes of four centuries, but also a chance to take guard again and consider how we can give the house and our custody of it the best chance to survive and prosper from now on.

Like Sam Goldwyn, I am wary of making predictions, particularly about the future. Certainly, if even the horizon scanners of the British Security establishment cannot forecast what will happen, the rest of us would do well to follow Goldwyn's advice. However, in order to survive and prosper it seems important, first to define our nature and purpose and, secondly, to be as clear as possible about risks and threats. We can then insure as best we can against them.

So, we must answer the question: what is Hatfield House for?

William Cecil, 1st Baron Burghley, 1520–1598, riding his grey mule. Artist unknown. Watercolour on paper 13 x 11 inches.

Robert Cecil, 1st Earl of Salisbury, 1563–1612, by John de Critz the Elder.

Print of a part of the interior of Theobalds, the house given to Robert Cecil by his father. James I exchanged it for Hatfield in 1607.

In 1611 there was no doubt about the answer. It was built to entertain the King, as we pursued our trade of high politics. Robert Cecil, the builder of Hatfield House, had been left Theobalds, an immense palace near Cheshunt, by his father, the great Lord Burghley, together with most of his estates south of the Trent. Robert Cecil, rather than his elder half-brother Thomas, Earl of Exeter, was Burghley's political heir, and he therefore needed bases and property in and near London, the centre of political power. Burghley had found Theobalds a convenient place to entertain Queen Elizabeth I, who liked to sponge off her rich subjects. His son, Robert, found it equally convenient for entertaining her successor, James I and VI. Unfortunately for Robert, but perhaps fortunately for his descendants, King James took a fancy to Theobalds and proposed to his Lord Treasurer that he should swap it for Hatfield, an old-fashioned fifteenth century palace, built by Cardinal Morton when he was Bishop of Ely. Queen Elizabeth had spent part of her childhood at Hatfield and had been confined there by her sister, Mary.

James I of England and VI of Scotland, by Paul van Somer.

Even Robert Cecil could not say no to the King and he therefore determined to make the best of a bad job. So, early in 1607, he rode over to inspect the place, conscious that if he were to maintain his position, he would still need to entertain the King, whether James possessed Theobalds or not. He pulled down three-quarters of Morton's palace and, aware of the need for speed, built the present house in just over four years. The House, together with the gardens, cost him £40,000, for comparison about 10% of the income of the English crown in 1603.

When it was finished, the House had taken the form of an E, perhaps a tribute to the late Queen, but, also, more practically, because its shape reflected its purpose. The east wing was for the King to occupy, the west wing was the Queen's. There was even an apartment in the centre for the hope of the Stuarts, Henry, Prince of Wales.

Sadly, the new house was never really used as its builder intended. Although the King dined there once, Robert Cecil died, agonisingly, of cancer, aged only 49, before he could occupy the House properly, let alone deploy it as part of the panoply of his power. Robert's son, William, was active in politics throughout his long incumbency (supporting Parliament against Charles I). However, he was never more than a relatively minor political figure, and he probably would have never risen to great eminence, even had he not been handicapped by his father's debts and his own extravagance.

During the family's eclipse in the seventeenth and eighteenth centuries, Hatfield remained the centre of a large, if somewhat encumbered, rural estate. Just before the 1688 Revolution, the Salisbury of the day, in an orgy of political incompetence and misjudgement, having flirted with the Whigs, not only rejoined the Tories, but turned Roman Catholic. Unsurprisingly, he landed in the Tower. He and his descendants remained Tories, so even if they had shown the interest and the ability, they could not have prospered during the long eighteenth century Whig ascendancy. It was only with the advent of the Irish Emily Mary at Hatfield and the Younger Pitt in Downing Street that Hatfield began to take on the role that the other great English country houses filled as a centre for the family's local 'interest' and as a source of power for political endeavour in the drawing rooms of London. As the family's political influence waxed again through the long nineteenth century into the dawn of the democratic age, the House's role as a centre of political influence waxed with it. It only finally relapsed into relative political

5th Marquess of Salisbury, 1893–1972, statesman and scholarly owner of Hatfield, who began to restore the house after the Second World War.

obscurity with the resignation of the 5th Marquess from Harold Macmillan's government in 1957.

In the twenty-first century it is unlikely that large country houses, even those as close to London as Hatfield, could ever play more than a walk-on part on the fringes of national politics. Politics has become the preserve, almost exclusively, of professional politicians who have done little else since before they sat their A-levels. In that they differ little from Lord Burghley, Robert Cecil or Prime Minister Salisbury. These days, however, running a house like Hatfield demands the establishment and management of capital assets sufficient to endow what often seems a bottomless financial pit. Unless the incumbent at Hatfield were to hand it over to the National Trust (which should only be a last resort) or depend on government grants (never enough and put not your trust in princes), he would never have the time to devote to both business and politics. Anyway, nowadays, one cannot simultaneously be a minister and a businessman.

Nevertheless, there is and should be a role for Hatfield. To survive and prosper any institution cannot be seen as an anachronism and Hatfield House is no exception. Since 1611 it has had to adapt itself to a changing world. It has done so partly because, whatever their idiosyncrasies, its custodians have nearly all wished it to survive and have enabled it to do so in their own way. There are, after all, as many ways of managing a large, privately-owned country house as there are custodians.

As this generation's custodians, how therefore do my wife and I see Hatfield's role as we launch it into its fifth century? The answer to the question could never be anything but subjective and personal, two adjectives that certainly describe what follows here.

The primary focus must remain the House and Park, with their associated buildings, gardens, lakes and rivers. John Cornforth wrote that the only original contribution the English have made to the arts is the English country house. The custodians of Hatfield are therefore the custodians of a work of art, not a perfect one, but an important one. So they must keep it in good order and, like their ancestors, add to its beauty, thereby preserving it, but also deepening the complexity of its patina. The dead hand of legislation, plus the heritage bureaucracy and lobby now make it impossible to alter the House, except by hanging movable objects on its walls. However, it is remarkable what improvements even such superficial changes can bring.

Equally, we can seek to add to our collections. Unlike Chatsworth or the many cupola'd Duke of Buccleuch, we have no great art collection, beyond a group of interesting portraits. We were too broke to spend anything on the Grand Tour and, by the nineteenth century, Prime Minister Salisbury was greeting his prospective daughter-in-law with the words: 'Welcome to Hatfield, which is Gaza, capital of Philistia.' However, we do have an interesting library and archive. On the whole, I am happier with that than with a Rembrandt or the odd Poussin. From time to time we have made modest purchases of books and pictures, not only for the pleasure of their beauty but also, in the case of contemporary works, to encourage young artists in the belief that, unless they grow, collections die.

As far as the Park is concerned, it is a place of magic, whose most remarkable feature is the astonishing number of veteran oaks that thrive there. As you will read later in this book, conserving these old ladies and gentlemen is something we take an increasing delight in.

One of the more careful judgements we have to make is over the question of public access. People love visiting the House and their comments are touchingly enthusiastic. At the same time, we are becoming increasingly aware of the cumulative effect of the tens of thousands of feet which have trooped through the place since it first opened to the public in 1948. We are unquestionably faced with the imperative of restricting numbers in future to preserve a structure that was flung up in a hurry and has been rickety ever since.

Luckily, modern technology and the West Wing will come to our aid. By 2016 we hope to have converted the ground floor and basement of the West Wing to exhibition space which its more solid Victorian construction will enable us to open for ten or eleven months a year. We will be able to show items there that have been hidden from public view: china, textiles, artefacts of empire, to take some examples.

Even more exciting to my mind, is the digitisation of our archive. We have entered into a partnership with ProQuest Ltd., who have now completed the first batch: a selection of over 30,000 letters, documents and maps from the sixteenth century. A terminal will make these available to our visitors for the first time and universities and libraries world-wide are beginning to show an interest in the project.

Just as the House suffers from visitor wear and tear, so does the Park. If you live within the ancient parish of Hatfield we welcome you all the year round, so long as you apply for a pass. The general public, however, do not visit the Park in the six months of autumn and winter. The poor old place gets enough of a hammering in the summer and, like our staff who look after it, it needs time to recover.

The question of access is also important for the family which lives at Hatfield. Our visitors constantly remark that one of the most attractive things about the house is that someone lives there. It is interesting that the present Chairman of the National Trust has recognized that that is one of the weaknesses of many of his properties. No one can live in a goldfish bowl, in spite of the flattering curiosity of our visitors about our habits and oddities. So, if we are to continue to live at Hatfield, the family needs to preserve a degree of privacy, or it would go collectively mad. Luckily, our visitors tend to be extraordinarily understanding about

OPPOSITE *The library was originally two rooms. The fireplace is original, but was moved from another position and altered to accommodate the mosaic portrait of Robert Cecil.*

The Chase Desk, commissioned for Hatfield in 2004 and made by Rupert Brown of Sixpenny Handley, Dorset. Its marquetry was made from veneer cut from 63 different trees in the neighbourhood of Cranborne.

what I would have expected to be a difficult thing for a casual tourist to comprehend.

Preserving the House and Park also depends on two other things. The first is having the money to keep them in good repair, and the second is that we contribute to the life of Hatfield and of Hertfordshire. To a marked degree these two things overlap.

We are lucky that Hatfield is still the centre of a substantial estate. Over the last few years we have formed a young and enthusiastic management team of high professionalism and infectious enthusiasm. They are rapidly transforming the businesses that support the House and Park. Buildings are being repaired and rebuilt to be re-let for new uses. Farms and woodlands are being efficiently managed and conservation programmes stepped up. Our businesses are diversifying to reduce our dependence on a single sector. We try and invest in new companies to encourage innovation.

Our results to date are encouraging, in spite of some worries about the recession. We are beginning to employ more local people, including some admirable seventeen and eighteen-year olds who, for some reason, had been previously thought unemployable. Our contractors are beginning to do the same.

We have also, in partnership with the University of Hertfordshire and a number of local businesses, begun to encourage thinking about how to improve the quality of development in our county, whose green belt is under particular pressure. In doing so we have encouraged the general public to participate in those discussions from the very beginning, rather than their first being consulted at a later stage. As a first practical step in this initiative, the Estate has held a series of public meetings, under the leadership of an international team of architects, to consider how those who live and work in Old Hatfield would like to see the less successful parts of the town improved. We have already begun to implement the recommendations that the people of Hatfield made as a result of those meetings.

I hope that over the next few years Hatfield will play host to a number of other projects as well.

We have plans to increase the number and scope of our educational programmes, building on the success of our 'Living History' days and establishing partnerships with local schools.

We would greatly enjoy holding more musical events and exhibitions. So we hope that this year's stunning Henry Moore exhibition is an earnest of things to come,

Stewart Johnston, one of the YMCA trainees who is currently working in the Building Department at Hatfield.

that Harry Christophers and The Sixteen and Nicholas Kok and Psappha will wish to return and that James MacMillan and Ben Foskett will hear the premières of more of their compositions played at Hatfield.

All of these things, the House and Park, the businesses, without which they could not exist, our attempts to make a contribution to local life and improve its quality will, I hope, enable a dispassionate observer to look at Hatfield House and say: 'We would miss it if it was not there.'

We will I hope, thus begin to be able to answer the question 'What is Hatfield for in 2011?'

Our successors' answers to the same question in 2111 will no doubt be different in detail. However, their answers will share at least one characteristic with ours. They will take a long-term view. Like ours, their businesses will be managed for the long term. Our relationship with our neighbours in Hatfield and Hertfordshire will be based on a mutual desire to make our part of the county as rewarding and as agreeable a place to live as possible for the long term. And, like us, their main difficulties will be caused by the bureaucracies, both British and European, which, oblivious to their own incompetence, will still see themselves as the masters rather than the servants.

A 400th anniversary is a time to be optimistic about the future. However, rapid change is overtaking our world. Economic power is rapidly moving east. Technology, for the moment, is giving unprecedented power to individuals and changing social structures.

A corrupt form of Islam is inducing panic in the West, leaching from us what remains of our power and self-confidence. Demography is causing a European crisis. Hatfield House will not be immune from these trends. All we can do is our best to insure against their worst effects and embrace any opportunities we can discern. So long as the House does not make you its slave, rather than its servant, there is no more enjoyable or rewarding occupation than being its custodians; and without enjoyment, there can be no success.

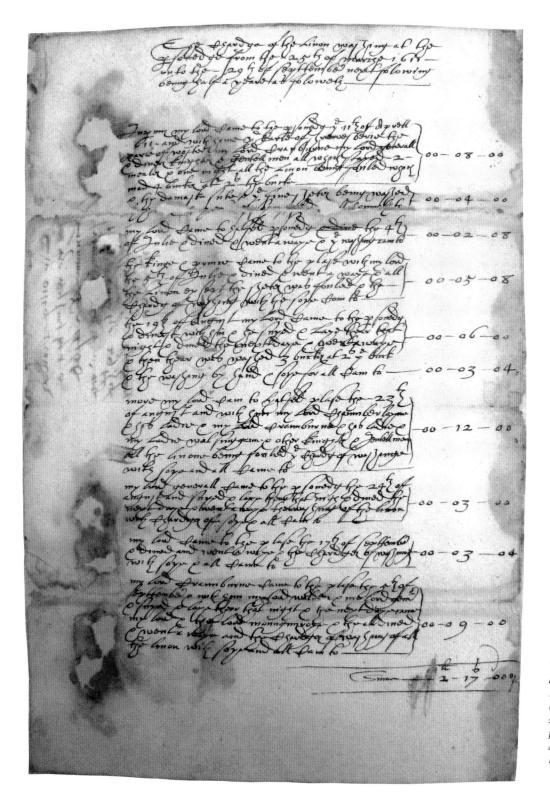

'The Chardge of the linen washing at the parsonadge . . .' The Parsonage Laundry Bill, 1611 (Bills 58/32). Damaged and scrappy-looking, this fragment of paper nevertheless tells us much about Robert Cecil's visits to Hatfield in 1611.

The Parsonage Laundry Bill and Robert Cecil's visit to Hatfield in 1611

ROBIN HARCOURT WILLIAMS

Robin Harcourt Williams has been Librarian and Archivist to the Marquess of Salisbury since 1972. He has edited the correspondence between the Third Marquess and his nephew A. J. Balfour, 1869–1892 Herts. Record Society 1988.

ROBERT CECIL'S papers at Hatfield House are an essential source for our national history. They include correspondence with almost everyone who exercised power and influence at the time, from the King downwards. In addition to these, there are to be found amongst the archives an enormous number of bills and accounts relating to the expenses of the Cecil household in the seventeenth century. They are trivial by comparison with the political papers but nevertheless are of interest for the light which they shed on ordinary, daily life. This brief study looks at bills relating to the year 1611 and is particularly concerned with Robert Cecil's visits to Hatfield when the building of his new house was nearing completion. Most of these visits took place during the half-year from 25 March until 29 September, which is the period covered by a bill for the washing of dirty linen at Hatfield Parsonage (hereinafter referred to as 'the laundry bill').

Hatfield Parsonage was used as a base by Robert Cecil, his children and senior officials during the five years that Hatfield House was being built. Conveniently situated a little more than half a mile distant, it was a house of considerable status. It was surrounded by nearly 100 acres of glebeland and had all the outbuildings which belong to a prosperous farm, including five large barns, a stable, a coach house, a dovecote and a brewhouse. Cecil was able to use the Parsonage because an Elizabethan rector had chosen not to live there and

had rented out the house, together with the tithes and glebeland, for a period of 99 years. Robert Cecil bought the lease for the remainder of its term. Much is known about the building, which probably dates to the late fifteenth century, because a survey and ground-floor plan of 1607 both exist. Like most new occupiers, Robert Cecil made it his first priority to build a new kitchen (Accounts 160/1 f. 48, 75).

The house had a sufficient number of good rooms to accommodate Lady Cranborne, Lady Francis Cecil, Lady Hume and their followers and attendants, numbering 42 people in all, for nine weeks in 1610 (Accounts 160/1 f. 93v.).

The laundry bill shows that Robert Cecil visited Hatfield six times between March and September 1611. The first occasion was on 11 April, when he came to the Parsonage accompanied by his son Lord Cranborne, his nephew Sir Edward Cecil, the Earls of Shrewsbury and Worcester and 'divers knights and gentlemen all which stayed two meals and one night, all the linen being fouled'. The Earl of Worcester would have been interested to have seen how building work was progressing, because he was one of the select group of three earls who had come with Robert Cecil on a visit to Hatfield four years earlier. Together they had viewed the ground and decided on the most suitable site for the new house. Sir Edward Cecil, a soldier who had served in the Netherlands – and who is described in the bill as 'my

Lord General' – owed much to his uncle's protection; a few months later he sent 1200 lime trees, which had been bought in France, to be planted at Hatfield (Box G/13 f. 20).

It is impossible to know how many people took part in this April visit but the number would not have been small. Whenever Robert Cecil travelled he was always accompanied by a large retinue. A list of provisions supplied for the two meals comprises 36 items (Bills 63). Similar lists survive in great numbers in the Hatfield archives and they show that a wide variety of different meats and fish were served at each meal. For the April visit, for instance, a dozen flounders, two carp, 18 great plaice, 200 cockles, 120 crayfish, and an eel were amongst the fish provided. There were also ample quantities of beef, mutton and lamb, six tame pigeons and a dozen wild pigeons, two calves' heads, 24 chickens and eight pullets. All this was washed down with claret wine, which was brought by the bottleman (Bills 67a/37).

For most of May and June Robert Cecil was based at his magnificent London residence, Salisbury House in the Strand, which had a garden running down to the Thames. There he had his own landing stage and his own barge. It presumably had six oarsmen, for a set of six new oars was bought on 2 June (Bills 64). £30.2.0 was spent in October on making a new barge, which cost almost as much again (£28) when it was painted by Cecil's ubiquitous decorator, Rowland Buckett (Box G/13 fols. 19v. & 56). The bargeman was Walter Snelling, whose bills (Bills 64) show that Cecil travelled up and down river almost daily during the early summer, usually going to the royal palace at Greenwich, to the Tower, or to Whitehall. Most of his official work was performed at Whitehall, where he also had his own bedroom and lodgings. He was criticised by some for monopolising power in his own hands, for he was not only Secretary of State and Master of the Court of Wards but also, from 1608 onwards, Lord High Treasurer as well. He was certainly overburdened with work and needed tireless energy, which sadly diminished as the year 1611 wore on.

The next visit to be recorded in the laundry bill occurred on 4 July, when 'my Lord came to Hatfield Parsonage and dined and went away'. At the time he was staying 10 miles away with the King at Theobalds, where he returned the same night. No doubt he had been preparing for the visit of the King and the Prince of

Three noble palaces: Salisbury House was situated between Durham House and Worcester House beside the River Thames in London. On their opposite side these mansions faced the Strand.

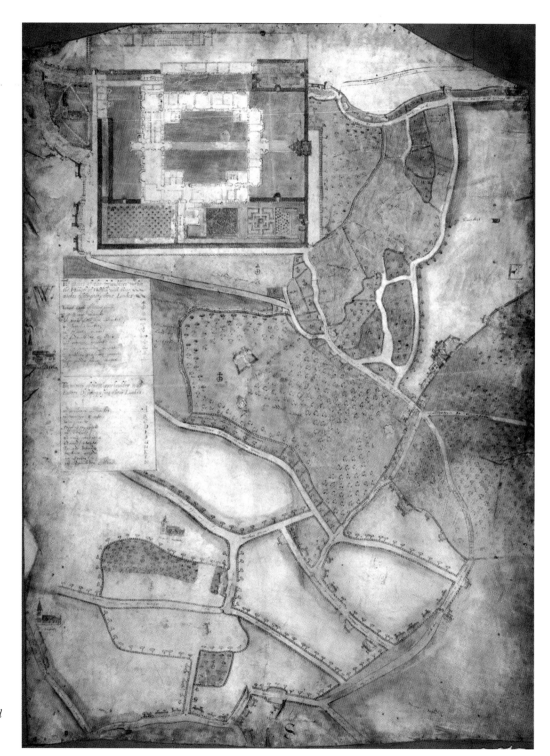

Map of Hatfield Park, about 1608, with an out-of-scale plan of the former royal manor house. Today called the Old Palace, it was known in Robert Cecil's time as The Place. Three of the four ranges shown surrounding the inner courtyard were pulled down when Hatfield House was built.

Wales, who 'came to the plase' the following day. (The Place was the old episcopal, and then royal, manor house at Hatfield which has been known since the 19th century as the Old Palace.) The wording of the bill suggests that the King ate in the Old Palace, rather than at the Parsonage. Hatfield House itself cannot yet have been sufficiently finished for the visitors to eat there; a report on the state of the work dated 1 July (BHH 84) shows how much remained to be done. The Old Palace originally consisted of four ranges surrounding a court-yard. The principal range, which contained the hall and the kitchen, is the only one which has survived, having been converted into stables in 1628/29. It appears that some of the building was pulled down in 1608 and one can only speculate whether the remaining wing would also have been demolished if Robert Cecil had lived longer. In any case, the hall and kitchen no doubt served a useful purpose during the King's visit.

The King not only inspected progress on the new building itself but also the gardens which were being laid out on the east and west sides of the house. The East Garden was particularly splendid, with terraces, parterres and a fountain. The fountain consisted of a statue, painted in polychrome by Rowland Buckett, of Neptune standing on a rock. The accounts record that the rock was altered twice 'against his Majesty came to Hatfield in July 1611' (Accounts 160/1 f. 153). Shortly after this the celebrated Huguenot engineer Salomon de Caus was employed to redesign the waterworks in the East Garden completely.

The design and layout of Hatfield House were entirely determined by the assumption that it would be visited often by the King and his court. The best apartments in the east and west wings were set aside for the King and Queen. In the event, the visit on 5 July was the only one which the King made in Robert Cecil's lifetime. The 2nd Earl of Salisbury by no means enjoyed his father's pre-eminent position in government and the King returned to Hatfield only once, on 15 June 1616, for the christening of Lord Salisbury's child. The King did not stay overnight on either of his visits.

Two weeks after the July visit, Robert Cecil spent several days at Windsor, where he went hunting with the King. Then at the beginning of August he joined the King on his summer progress into Surrey, Hampshire and Wiltshire. Cecil was accompanied by, amongst others, his cook and his sculleryman, a page, porters and several grooms. A bottleman and his assistant came too, with three horses and a cart loaded with beer and wine; a constant supply of drink was essential when the cleanliness of local water was a matter of doubt. Two carts were hired to carry Cecil's luggage, which included beds and bedroom hangings, as well as trunks for holding state papers. A coachman and his boy were in charge of five horses and a heavy, lumbering coach. No wonder that when Cecil stayed at Windsor in July, stabling had to be found for 30 of his horses: 14 at The Talbot and 16 at The Lion (Bills 65). Considering that the King led the progress accompanied by his own waggons and servants, and was followed by other great courtiers with their retinues, the disruption caused by all of them combined can only be imagined.

Forming part of Cecil's entourage were always several 'footmen': men who travelled on foot, usually running, who were available to deliver messages and undertake errands. Numerous claims for expenses submitted by the footmen show that almost every day they dispensed small sums in charity on Cecil's behalf, wherever he went. On the August progress, for example, a shilling was given 'to the prisoners at Salisbury' and a shilling 'to the almshouse at Sarum'. More was given 'to two poor soldiers on the way' and 'to two hospitals on the way' (Bills 67/36). Somewhat improbably, on more than one occasion earlier in the year a shilling had been given 'to the poor at Knightsbridge' (Bills 64). One claim is strikingly imprecise: in June 1611 Cecil's man Francis Rogers successfully asked to be reimbursed 20 shillings which he had 'laid out to Archie the [King's] jester at Windsor' and 2s. 6d 'laid out but for what I cannot well tell, my memory being my adversary' (Bills 64).

On 8 August Robert Cecil left Salisbury for a short visit to his manor house at Cranborne in Dorset. He entertained the King there the following day. There too Cecil was engaged in building operations, having

Cranborne Manor in Dorset, where Robert Cecil entertained the King during the summer progress of 1611.

already made important additions to what had been a mediaeval hunting lodge. Well situated as a base for hunting in Cranborne Chase, the house proved to be particularly attractive to King James, who had already stayed there in 1609 and was to return a number of times in the future. In 1611 William Arnold, the mason, was building a new terrace and kitchen at Cranborne Manor and, as at Hatfield, much new planting was taking place in the gardens. If this were not enough, Cecil was also concurrently enlarging the garden at Salisbury House in London and constructing a second mansion, known as Little Salisbury House, next to the principal one.

After spending the first fortnight of August taking part in the royal progress, Cecil returned to London. On 19 August, according to the laundry bill, 'my Lord came to the Parsonage and divers with him. He supped and lay there that night and dined the next day and went away . . . More my lord came to Hatfield Place the 23th of August and with him my Lord Chamberlain and his Lady and my Lord Cranborne and his Lady and my Lady Walsingham and other knights and gentlemen'. The Lord Chamberlain was the Earl of Suffolk, father of

Lady Cranborne and Cecil's successor as Lord Treasurer. Between 1603 and 1616 he built a gigantic palace at Audley End. He was another of the three earls who had come to Hatfield in 1607 to help Cecil choose where to build his new house.

Other sources disagree with the date of 23 August which is given in the laundry bill. It is not unusual to discover that, out of so many bills surviving in the archives which were often submitted by relatively illiterate servants, some differ slightly over dates or that figures have been wrongly added up. Robert Cecil could not have been at Hatfield on 23 August because he stayed most of the week at Sir Walter Cope's house in Kensington and two of his footmen, John Richardson and Anthony Errington, made separate claims for 'drinking money' of one shilling for 'going with my Lord from Kensington to Oatlands' in Surrey on 23 August. They each received another shilling for returning with their master from the Queen's palace at Oatlands to Kensington the following day. On 25 August they both accompanied Robert Cecil from Kensington to Hatfield and left the next day for Audley End. Predictably there is also a bill from the bottleman, confirming that he 'went with my Lord's drink' to Hatfield on 25 August and to Audley End the day after. Other bills show that five grooms attended Cecil during the visit, as well as the coachman and his boy. Amongst the provisions supplied on 25 August were not only partridges, quails and wild pigeons but also two dozen sparrows (Bills 63). Incidentally, blackbirds really were eaten: seven were sent to Robert Cecil at court, together with woodcock, green plover and snipe, on 16 December. Another half dozen blackbirds followed them four days later (Bills 63).

The laundry bill notes that the Lord General, Sir Edward Cecil, stayed at Hatfield Parsonage on the night of 24 August and dined there the next day. On 29 August Robert Cecil returned from Audley End to Hatfield and ate two meals there. The final entry in the laundry bill refers to a visit to the Old Palace which was made the following week. 'My Lord Cranborne came to the Place the 5th of September & with him my Lord

The Long Gallery at Hatfield, with its original Jacobean plaster ceiling and carved panelling. The chimney pieces were not finished until 1612.

Walden & my Lord General and supped & lay there that night & the next day came my Lord & the Lord Montgomery & they all dined & went away and the charges of washing of all the linen with soap and all came to 9 shillings.'

It is unfortunate that the laundry bill only covers the half-year ending on 29 September 1611 and we have no similar record of visits made by Cecil to Hatfield after that date. He certainly came at least once more, for in a different account book we read of a payment of £5.4.4 made 'to William Lewis upon two bills for provisions of diet for your honour at Hatfield the 4th and 5th of October 1611' (Box G/13).

There is good reason to suppose that by this time work on the house was close enough to being finished for Cecil to have slept in it. A report on the state which the work had reached by 1 July, just before the King's visit (BHH 84) shows that much remained to be done but a great deal of progress had been made by 30 September, when inventories were taken of the contents of Hatfield House and the Parsonage (Box A/1). It is clear that by this time most of the rooms in Hatfield House were furnished with tables, beds and carpets. The kitchen was well-stocked with pie plates, dishes, brass pots and copper kettles. There were a few paintings on the wall and many of the grander rooms were hung with tapestries. In Robert Cecil's panelled bedroom stood a bedstead made of walnut with a tester, valance and headpiece of crimson velvet. Cecil's coat of arms was embroidered on the headpiece. Five 'tapestry hangings of imagery' decorated the walls and in the room there were a high chair, a stool, a table and a cupboard. There was just one picture: a portrait of his mother.

The next report on the progress of building work dates from January 1612 (BHH 88). The house was certainly not complete. Two wooden chimney pieces in the Long Gallery remained to be carved and painted and joiners still had to fit wainscot and chimney pieces in several other rooms. Some bedrooms were being altered with partitions, the decoration of the chapel was not finished and there was a great deal of work to be done on lodges and outbuildings. However one has the

The rambling former Parsonage at Hatfield, parts of which date to the late 15th century. Robert Cecil, his children and senior officials stayed here while Hatfield House was being built.

impression that Cecil would have stayed in the house if he had had the opportunity to make a visit.

Unfortunately he became increasingly ill during the autumn and winter of 1611. In August he was checked by the King's doctor, Theodore Mayerne, and from then onwards he consulted in addition numerous other doctors with increasing desperation until the time of his death. His declining state of health is indicated in the accounts by payments such as those made on 13 December of £2 for 'a black taffeta scarf with gold lace for my Lord to carry his arm' (Bills 62) and on 23 December 'for wormwood beer for my Lord when he was sick' (Bills 67/21). The upholsterer's bill for work done over the following months makes agonizing reading: not only were wooden crutches made, covered with red cloth, but also an armchair of walnut with four wheels. It had elbow rests and rests under the armpits which were padded with feathers; more and more feathers and padding were added in successive stages, in a vain attempt to counteract the intense pain which Cecil was evidently suffering.

In one last search for a cure, Cecil travelled to Bath in the spring of 1612 and died at Marlborough on 24 May, on his way back to London. He was aged only 49. It is poignant that, after all the care which he had taken over the building of Hatfield, Cecil did not live to inhabit it. If his life had not been cut short, he would most probably welcomed the King and the court to his new house with a lavish entertainment, no doubt staged by Inigo Jones and with speeches written by Ben Jonson, as he had previously done both at Theobalds and at Salisbury House. But in the event, although the laundry bill confirms that he made regular visits to the site and saw Hatfield House when it was almost finished, it remains unproven whether he ever actually stayed a night in it.

As for the Parsonage, it became simply the home farm and brewery for Hatfield House before reverting to the Rector of Hatfield later in the seventeenth century. Having been replaced by a new rectory in 1889, it was used as a county primary school in the second half of the twentieth century. More recently the house and grounds were sold for private development and about a year ago the former Parsonage was converted into a nursing home with 29 bedrooms – rooms which for a brief period had been occupied by some of the greatest in the land.

Robert Cecil and James I

PAULINE CROFT

Pauline Croft is Professor of Early Modern History at Royal Holloway University of London and senior convenor of the Tudor-Stuart research seminar at the Institute of Historical Research, University of London. She is editor of, and a contributor to, Patronage Culture and Power: the Early Cecils *and author of* King James.

IN 1598, as Lord Burghley sickened, Elizabeth I sent a message thanking him for bringing up his son Robert 'as near as may be like unto yourself'. Cecil became a Privy Counsellor in 1591, aged 28, and on Burghley's death he was left with the problem of the succession. The Queen's closest relative was King James VI of Scotland, but she would not confirm him as her heir. Instead, there grew up a cult of Elizabeth the ageless beauty, epitomised by the extraordinary Rainbow portrait, commissioned by Cecil around 1600 and probably by Marcus Gheeraerts. In reality the ageing Queen was struggling to cope with exceptional difficulties. War continued, despite the defeat of the Spanish Armada in 1588. In Ireland, a great revolt was master-minded after 1595 by the formidable Tyrone, who defeated successive English forces despatched against him. Four failed harvests in a row between 1594 and 1598 sent English food prices soaring, with terrible consequences for the urban poor. In September 1600, Elizabeth was 67. Her grandfather King Henry VII had died at 62, and her father Henry VIII at 56. Gloriana was a fading relic of her former greatness.

North of the Border, the Scottish King James VI was increasingly obsessed by his claim to the English throne. The only child of Mary Queen of Scots, James was directly descended from Henry VII, but in law his claim to the English throne was not entirely clear. James feared that the Cecils still preferred the English-born descendants of Henry VIII's sister Princess Mary Tudor. James turned to the Earl of Essex, Elizabeth's last favourite, who became his informant on English politics. Essex was anxious to reinforce the King's mistrust of Cecil, but the earl's abortive revolt in London in 1601 and his execution thereafter, forced James to re-think his position.

The King needed the assurance that on Elizabeth's demise his claim would be immediately backed by the Privy Council. By 1601 Cecil was Elizabeth's most influential adviser and her Principal Secretary of State. James sardonically described him as 'king there in effect', not a phrase he would use lightly. Scottish envoys arrived in London in spring 1601, and after some fruitless audiences with Elizabeth, they made contact with Cecil. He indicated that in due course, he would support the Scottish succession. Cecil managed to increase the pension already paid to James, although he had some difficulty in persuading Elizabeth to part with the money. Then he discreetly joined in the secret correspondence that some Englishmen were already conducting with the Scottish king.

In March 1603, realising the end was near, Cecil drafted the proclamation to announce Elizabeth's death and the transfer of her crown 'absolutely, wholly, and solely' to James. The ports were closed and London was under extra watch. However, there was no sign of

OPPOSITE *The Rainbow portrait of Queen Elizabeth I, painted in about 1600.*

trouble, although the proclamation of James' accession on the morning of 24 March was received with apparent bemusement, described tactfully by one diarist as 'silent joy'. On 27 March 1603 James wrote to Cecil praising him and his fellow-councillors for their care in overseeing the transition. Acknowledging Cecil's crucial role, he added, 'How happy I think myself by the conquest of so wise a counsellor I reserve it to be expressed out of my own mouth unto you'. Cecil would keep the administration of England ticking over until the King's arrival.

James rode south, feasting and hunting, revelling in the crowds who flocked to see him. However, much of the warmth of their greeting was coloured by relief that the old Queen's death had not been followed by invasion and civil war. Cecil rode north to meet the King at York. There is no record of what they discussed, although foreign policy must have been high on the agenda. Cecil returned to prepare his great house at Theobalds for the King before he made his entry into London.

James had worked for years to win the English throne. He intended, as the Venetian ambassador ironically noted 'to enjoy the papacy . . . [and] dedicate himself to his books and to the chase'. What would come to Cecil? Royal gratitude might prove short-lived. Although Cecil retained the Principal Secretaryship of State, perhaps in future he would be only one of a dozen principal advisers. His position as master of the Court of Wards was not immediately confirmed, among rumours that James was considering bestowing the lucrative office elsewhere. Other noblemen were immediately given earldoms, and the Earl of Southampton, kept in the Tower since his involvement in Essex's rebellion, was freed and awarded the Garter. In May 1603, considering the membership of his Privy Council, the King wished to add members of 'the ancient nobility, whose birth and merit make them more capable than others'. The upstart Cecil was given merely a barony and even in 1604, after negotiating the treaty with Spain that ended the Armada war, only a viscountcy.

The nightmare possibility was that the King's initial gratitude would wane. James brought with him a group

The Ermine portrait of Queen Elizabeth I, painted in 1585, attributed to Nicholas Hilliard.

of Scottish friends and advisers who took over the Bedchamber, the innermost court circle that waited personally on the King. Lavish rewards began to flow their way. However, it became apparent that real power would not follow the royal generosity. By 1604 James' initial plans for a Union between England and Scotland were clearly unacceptable. The elites of each country would remain separate, and although a handful of Scots became privy counsellors, they held few English offices.

At some point in spring 1603, Cecil wrote a tract on the office of the Principal Secretary, revived by Elizabeth. The secretary saw the monarch regularly, usually daily, and success depended on the personal rapport between sovereign and servant. Much of the tract's language of courtly love reflected an earlier Elizabethan style. Startlingly, Cecil compares the secret councils between the prince and the secretary to 'the mutual affections of two lovers, undiscovered to their friends.' If the relationship soured, the secretary's position would become untenable: 'a suspicion of a Secretary is both a trial and a condemnation, and a judgment.' With a typical touch of irony, Cecil concluded that 'He that lives at mercy ought to be careful in the choice of his master'. In effect, in 1601 Cecil had done just that – chosen his future master.

Cecil's struggle to retain his pre-eminence was successful. Two unexpected factors assisted him: the King's passion for hunting, allied to his almost immediate dislike of London. By 1605, James was spending months at a time at his favourite hunting lodges of Royston and Newmarket. Someone must oversee the flood of government paperwork in the King's absence, and Cecil alone was capable of handling the sheer range and quantity of business demanding daily attention. James' confidence in him rose steadily. In their correspondence, Cecil became the king's 'little beagle', going ahead and sniffing out the terrain. Cecil did not care for the hunting epithet, but as long as it was a royal term of endearment, he put up with it. It was an indication of his renewed grasp on power that in 1605 he became Earl of Salisbury, at last catching up with his rivals, and in 1606, a Knight of the Garter. This exceptional honour led him to plan an ostentatious procession to Windsor that equalled if not exceeded the coronation procession itself.

It quickly became apparent that James' chief weakness was his extravagance. His generosity to his Scots was in part an investment in keeping them loyal. Absentee kingship might be perilous, and James could not afford to allow Scotland to become discontented, even rebellious, in his absence. However, just as in Scotland, James was renowned for giving to whomever badgered him most winningly, in England he showered gifts on Scotsmen without much discrimination, mostly to those who were at James' beck and call in the Bedchamber, rather than the men most vital to the smooth running of his native kingdom. Meanwhile in England, there was a

Double portrait of two Lord Treasurers: William Cecil, Lord Burghley, and Robert Cecil, Earl of Salisbury.

rising tide of anger at his growing indebtedness. The first Parliament of the reign assembled in March 1604, but was prorogued in July after declining to vote any taxation. The Privy Council met regularly to try to diminish the King's debts and increase revenues, since the ordinary receipts were failing to cover expenses. Once he was secure in his regained position as chief minister, Cecil began to broach the financial crisis with the King: the little beagle was biting back. In July 1605 the Privy Council wrote a formal letter, urging James in future to be more restrained in his giving, which bred 'great distraction and scandal'. Drafted for the Privy Council by Robert Cecil as Principal Secretary (and occasionally relapsing into the first person singular), the letter brought James to a greater awareness of his debts, but its effect was only temporary.

In 1608, the death of the Earl of Dorset, who had followed Burghley as Lord Treasurer in 1598, allowed the King to add a third major office to the two that Cecil already held as Principal Secretary and Master of the Court of Wards. The promotion triggered one of the most extraordinary family portraits, the posthumous painting of Burghley together with his son, each holding the Lord Treasurer's staff of office. It deliberately recalled the earlier great portrait of Burghley alone with his staff. Now his son took on the immense responsibility of restraining the King's indebtedness and restoring the English monarchy to solvency. Cecil unleashed a whirlwind of activity in the Treasury, where he found a morass of unsorted paperwork. Tirelessly he sat in judgment, despatching the backlog and getting to grips with the ruinous state of the King's finances. In his first two months he signed nearly three thousand letters and recovered £37,455 for the King's revenues.

Yet the main challenge was not to reform the Treasury, but rather to reform the King. In 1609 Cecil began work on a series of tough-talking treatises intent on making James face reality. The Lord Treasurer employed extraordinary bluntness in trying to bring him to a recognition that his extravagance was a fundamental cause of the financial problems. Cecil acknowledged the burdens under which the English state laboured in the 1590s, and the problems that Elizabeth had encountered in funding a lengthy war. Yet all that was needed afterwards was a period of common-sense economy and recuperation. Instead, James consumed his revenues and scattered his bounty. Cecil pointed to Henry VII, expressing his admiration for the frugal, hard-working monarch, 'who being not born to a kingdom . . . framed himself to such frugality as was far under a King of England.' This was a pointed example since it was from Henry VII that James derived his claim to the English throne. Cecil showed his distaste for the flamboyant Henry VIII, 'who thought all things lawful' where money was concerned, and became 'the poorest son of the richest father that ever this land had'. Henry was only saved from financial disaster by the Dissolution of the Monasteries, a recourse not open to James.

Cecil attacked the royal household, where the King's servants were 'a little army compared to former times'. There was only one course of action. 'It is not possible for a King of England, much less of Great Britain . . . to be rich or safe,' wrote Cecil, 'but by frugality'. England was rich only when contrasted with hardscrabble Scotland, not when contrasted with the wealthy Low Countries or the kingdoms ruled by Henri IV of France or Philip III of Spain. Cecil pointed out that Elizabeth

herself, that paragon of frugality, had been hard put to steer the English throne through the gravely over-stretched 1590s, a period he could vividly remember.

Unlike James in his published works, Cecil did not comment on the theoretical powers of monarchy. 'I think it such a kind of sacrilege to dispute of the power of the King' he wrote graciously. The key point was whether 'the practice be seasonable for the time . . . time is a great commander in the affairs of men.' Cecil knew that James was exulting in what he saw as the vastly greater resources of his new monarchy, when on the contrary, in 1603 the English crown was financially exhausted by war. 'Your Majesty may therefore please to remember first that you found a people worn with great and heavy burdens.'

Cecil alluded to the King's excessive bounty, much of it showered on Scots. He emphasised that he would defend the King's countrymen firmly in Parliament against any disrespectful criticisms, or as he put it, 'any frivolous objection.' The solution was to put the Scots on suitable pensions, 'a yearly maintenance to private men of Your Majesty's nearest retinue'. If the Commons thought that a better solution would be to send the Scots home, the riposte would be to ask if James should go back to Scotland as well. The thought that Edinburgh, not London, might become the capital of Great Britain would be enough to quell any such objections.

Cecil was deferential towards the Scots, but he was desperate to make James realise the urgency of the situation. There were no financial reserves in the Exchequer. 'This I write with dolour but have beheld with fear and terror.' It was the Lord Treasurer's duty to face his master with the unpalatable facts, 'showing you demonstrably how the storm comes before it breaks.' If the King would only take action, Cecil like the aged Simeon seeing the infant Christ, could say, 'Nunc Dimittis'. However, Cecil was not merely urging economies; he had a plan, although it might not be entirely agreeable to the King. James was quickly disillusioned with the English Parliament, which in 1604 had shown no interest in his great project for Anglo-Scottish Union. Cecil was also acutely aware that the Commons believed that

English taxation was intended to fund the necessities of the realm, not the King's private extravagances.

Peace with Spain had been one of the greatest joint achievements of James and Cecil, but it had its downside. Heavy taxation in peacetime was unusual: 'peace was ever a calm to the people'. Cecil urged the King to recognise that there was no escaping the political centrality of the English Parliament, 'to which power all men yield an implicit obedience.' It would be far better to risk allowing a Parliament to discuss the King's finances than to go on money-raising by relying on non-parliamentary means, which was 'full of inconveniences'.

After becoming Lord Treasurer in 1608, Cecil had spent two years reforming the Exchequer, driving down the King's debts and devising a scheme to restore financial stability. The treatises he was writing were intended to prepare the King for that plan, later known as the Great Contract, for a fundamental re-structuring the royal finances with parliamentary assistance.

Cecil was also planning to combine his proposals for reforming Crown finance with a parliamentary celebration for the creation of the sixteen-year-old Prince Henry as Prince of Wales. There had not been a grown Prince of Wales since Arthur, son of Cecil's hero Henry VII, and Henry was already seeking conferment of his title. The King would have to grant the Prince a household of his own, which would be another burden on the exchequer. Since Henry's enhanced role was unavoidable, the best strategy was to stage the Prince's creation within a public, parliamentary setting. The event might rekindle that sense of gratitude for the Stuart succession which had been so strong in 1603. By 1610, James' popularity was on the wane, but Cecil would present Henry, who embodied James' supreme advantage over the childless Elizabeth. England had welcomed not only a new king but a dynasty, the royal 'olive branches' of King James and Queen Anne's offspring. That should encourage financial generosity. The ceremony did indeed present Henry in princely splendour, and was rendered all the more poignant by the shocking news of the assassination of Henri IV. Just as France was plunged into a dangerous minority, England could rejoice in the stability provided by the future prospect of 'Henry IX'.

In Parliament, Cecil pointed to the inevitable costs of supporting a royal family, not just a spinster Queen. He noted unavoidable charges such as the King's coronation and the welcome required for ambassadors coming to congratulate the new monarch. He emphasised the dangers to peace and stability if it became known that the King of Great Britain was so poor that he could not defend his country against invasion, or support his merchants abroad. There was a real threat to the realm as a whole if the Crown was perceived as weakened by the Stuart succession. Here was the difference between the public and the private spheres. Cecil was extraordinarily blunt in writing his treatises, which have no parallel in English history. These were only for the private sphere, in which he wrote confidentially (and critically) to the monarch. The public sphere was very different. Cecil was a seasoned politician, well aware that it was an essential part of his task to present the King's financial problems in the best possible light in Parliament.

Despite all Cecil's skills of presentation, the Great Contract failed, and for a while James was furious. 'There is no more trust to be laid upon this rotten reed of Egypt' (the House of Commons) he fumed. Cecil had been 'a little blinded with the self-love of your own counsel in holding together this parliament.' But rather like Burghley after the execution of Mary Queen of Scots, Cecil's period out of royal favour was brief. Like Burghley, he was indispensable, and by January 1611 James had returned to his usual practice of channelling virtually all business through the Secretary.

It is ironic that during these years, when Cecil put his career on the line, first with his blunt treatises then with the inherently risky Great Contract, he was also building a great house designed to receive the King, the Queen and the court. The Lord Treasurer was intent on maintaining the public image of grandeur, both for himself and his King. Just as Burghley built Theobalds, so Cecil built Hatfield, to welcome the monarch. As one of his obituarists was to comment, Cecil was 'a courtier from his cradle', and he had all the courtier's skills of ingratiation.

Hatfield was relatively small for a prodigy house, and far less rambling than Theobalds. It made up for lack of size by the sheer sumptuousness of the interior and the comfortable living accommodation made possible by its compact plan.

The royal image at Hatfield was embodied in statuary. The grandly dominating image of James strides out from the drawing-room mantelpiece. Bronze would have been far too heavy, so the statue is carved in wood, gilded to imitate classical bronzes, in fashion as collectors' items. Throughout the house, Cecil insisted on the highest craftsmanship, as can be seen in the magnificent Marble Hall and the astonishingly carved Great Staircase, a masterpiece of English woodworking.

Hatfield was built with remarkable speed, and in summer 1611 it was finished.

That summer, the King came to visit but only for the day: Cecil must have hoped for longer visits in future. That same summer he consulted the King's doctor, Sir Theodore Mayerne, whose extensive case notes indicate that the patient had cancer. Cecil managed to continue to work until the end of the year, December 1611, when he handed over the day-to-day running of the Exchequer to his devoted subordinate Sir Julius Caesar. Near to his end, in spring 1612 Cecil made a visit to Bath to ease his pains, where he received lavish presents from the King and Queen with their warm wishes for his recovery, but he died in May 1612. His tomb was his last great commission, an austere masterpiece by Maximilian Colt. The four cardinal virtues hold the slab with the Lord Treasurer in his garter robes and Lord Treasurer's staff, but there is no inscription extolling his remarkable career. Instead, underneath, is a gisant, a skeleton, indicating that all worldly power ends with death. Cecil was often weary of the court, and he died knowing that he had not succeeded in convincing James that an English monarch could only be rich, and safe, by frugality. As he had presciently told the King, he wanted to show him 'how the storm comes, before it breaks'. It is hard not to conclude that already, by 1612, Robert Cecil feared that the Stuart dynasty would one day reap the harvest of financial fecklessness sown by James I.

OPPOSITE *Statue of King James I by Maximilian Colt. It stands over the chimney piece in King James's Drawing Room.*

RIGHT *Tomb of Robert Cecil, carved by Maximilian Colt, in Hatfield parish church.*

Music in the Household of Robert Cecil

LYNN HULSE

Lynn Hulse FSA trained as a musicologist and has a doctorate from King's College, London. She has published numerous articles and essays on the role of music in the sixteenth and seventeenth century English noble households. She is currently Tutor in Contextual Studies at the Royal School of Needlework.

THE MUSICIANS' gallery at the east end of Hatfield's Marble Hall together with the series of carved musical putti that decorate the grand staircase serve to remind today's visitors of the house's illustrious musical past under the patronage of its builder, Robert Cecil, Earl of Salisbury.

Cecil's passion for and knowledge of music were well known among his contemporaries. According to the lutenist John Dowland, Cecil 'royally entertain[ed] the Exercise of Musicke', and the patronage that he extended to 'many professors' of the art was widely commented upon in print. Sir Michael Hickes, his father's secretary, first encouraged Cecil to establish a consort within his own household. We know from the records preserved in the archive at Hatfield that between about 1591 and his death in 1612 Cecil employed around twenty professional musicians and apprentices, including three members of the renowned Lanier family (John, Innocent and Nicholas), the court singer Robert Hales, the viol player Giovanni Coprario and the Irish harpist Cormack MacDermott (see Table).

From 1607 (the first year for which detailed accounts survive), Cecil maintained a permanent consort of two boys and three to five men. Whilst it is true that a number of late Elizabethan and early Jacobean aristocratic households could assemble a group of singers

and/or instrumentalists, some of its members were either competent amateurs gathered from within the ranks of family servants or professional musicians borrowed temporarily from relatives and friends or hired from the Court. It was unusual to find a professional consort on the scale of Cecil's in full-time private service. The only other patron known to have employed a group of comparable size and status was his 'most special and deerest friend', Thomas Sackville, 1st Earl of Dorset. As well as the permanent members in Cecil's consort, at least seven other adult musicians, four of whom were employed in the royal household, served on a part-time or occasional basis.

The relationship between patron and musician was no different from that of any other household servant. In addition to clothing, board and lodging, musicians were entitled to an annual wage, traditionally paid quarterly at Lady Day, Midsummer, Michaelmas and Christmas. The sum varied from as little as 40s (£2) to 40 marks (£26.67) per annum. The permanent members of Cecil's consort received £20 a year plus occasional gifts, a level of remuneration enjoyed by few musicians in private employment and only by Cecil's most senior retainers. It was not unusual for household musicians to suffer from arrears of pay. Martin Otto, for example, whose wages were nearly three years overdue, was forced to exercise the right to distrain, and in 1608 he demanded from his master, Gilbert Talbot, 7th Earl of Shrewsbury, a chest of viols and a bed in settlement of

OPPOSITE *The Musicians Gallery in the Marble Hall at Hatfield, built in 1611.*

39

Musical putto from the grand staircase, Hatfield, 1611.

non-payment. Unlike Shrewsbury, Cecil paid promptly in the belief that his servants should have no excuse to fail in their duty.

Boy musicians in private service were bound by the law of indenture. In most crafts or trades youths entered an apprenticeship in their late teens and served the statutory minimum term of seven years, but the demand for treble voices and the need to train musicians from an early age led many masters to indenture young boys. Two of Cecil's apprentices, Simon (?Ives) and George Mason, probably began their indenture at the age of eight and nine years respectively. However, in order to obtain the most experienced singers, masters tended to appoint boys who had received their initial training elsewhere. Cecil was no exception. In August 1595 he was eager to acquire Sir Richard Champernown's apprentice whose voice was 'farr in deede beyond his desert'. Threatened with exposure at Court for allegedly castrating boys to preserve their voices, Champernown appealed to Cecil for help, only to find the latter determined to obtain the apprentice for himself. At first Champernown refused to part with him on the grounds that he had gained 'smale or no contentment but yn musick' in return for the time and money spent on the boy's education, and that the quality of his consort would be severely impaired by the loss, but reflecting further on the matter, he judiciously offered the singer to Cecil a month at a time 'for yowr pryvate contentment'.

As in other professions, the master contracted to instruct his apprentice and to provide him with board, lodging and clothing for the duration of his indenture. By the late sixteenth century boys were taught musical theory and a variety of practical skills, including singing and playing on bowed and plucked instruments. Cecil's apprentices were taught primarily to sing and to play on the lute and viol by the brothers John and Innocent Lanier, who received an annual fee of £20 for the

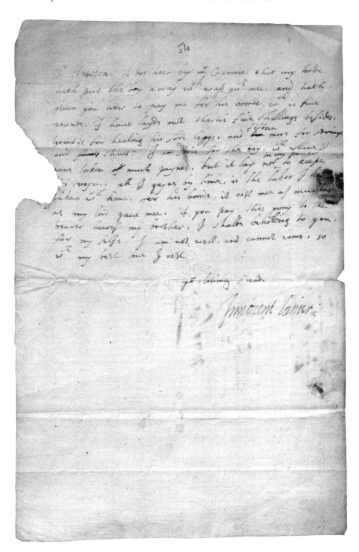

Letter from Innocent Lanier to Cecil's steward, Richard Houghton, regarding the singing boy, George Mason, August 1608: 'I am sorie for the boy, with whome I have taken much paynes, but it lay not in my power to keep his voyce'.

instruction and board of each boy. However, some of the more accomplished apprentices received extra tuition from specialist tutors. For example, Cecil's Danish instrumentalist, Christian Crusse, who may have been a gift from Christian IV of Denmark, entertained at Theobalds in July 1606, and studied for a year with the viol player Joseph Sherley.

Household service protected musicians from punishment as vagabonds but it did not entitle them to claim immunity from other aspects of the law, though masters could and sometimes did intervene to protect their servants from prosecution. In 1608 Henry Oxford, a viol player in Cecil's consort, was dismissed for allegedly kidnapping a woman 'of substance' and forcing her to marry against her will, a felony that carried a minimum sentence of two years' imprisonment. (It appears from the available evidence that the abduction had actually been an elopement.) Dismissal from the household of England's leading statesman severely impaired his chances of employment elsewhere so Oxford was obliged to secure Cecil's forgiveness and regain his protection. Hickes agreed to intercede on the musician's behalf, citing in his defence a bass singer whose 'base condicions' Cecil had condoned because 'your delight in the rareness of his voyce spurd yow on both to allow him an honorable pencion and to beare with many his imperfections.' Initially Cecil retorted, 'I can judge it fitter for me to quitt my love of Musique which pleaseth myne eare then to protect leudnes in this kind,' but he seems to have mellowed, using his position as Secretary of State to protect Oxford; the musician was reinstated to the consort a few months later.

The scope for advancement within private service was limited. A musical apprentice on completion of his indenture might be promoted within the household to the rank of paid servant as in the case of Crusse, though not all of Cecil's apprentices were so fortunate. When Mason's voice broke at the age of fourteen he was deemed surplus to requirement and was passed on to Cecil's son-in-law, Henry Lord Clifford, for the remaining two years of his indenture.

For employees in the household of the Secretary of

State, the only advancement open to Cecil's adult musicians lay in royal service. MacDermott left the consort sometime before October 1605 to join the King's Musick, but he continued to play on a part-time basis and was held in such high esteem that he accompanied Cecil on his final journey to Bath shortly before the latter's death on 24 May 1612. Two other household musicians asked for Cecil's support in the hope of securing royal office. In July 1605 John Lanier attempted to secure Piero Guye's place in the royal wind band for his son Nicholas, one of Cecil's apprentices. Lanier had occupied the post for twenty years in Guye's absence, and

---

TABLE: ROBERT CECIL'S MUSICIANS AND APPRENTICES

	Known dates of employment	*Instrument/voice*
MUSICIANS IN FULL-TIME SERVICE		
Christopher Heybourne	1591 - July 1598	instrumentalist
Cormack MacDermott	Feb. 1603 - Oct. 1605	Irish harp
Nicholas Lanier	Oct. 1607 - May 1612	singer/viol/lute/flute
Henry Oxford	Oct. 1607 - May 1612	viol/?singer
William Frost	Oct. 1607 - Dec. 1611	virginal
Thomas Warwick	Mar. 1608 - Mar. 1609	organ/virginal
Christian Crusse	Jan. 1611 - May 1612	viol/?singer
Unidentified musician	dead by April 1608	bass singer
MUSICIANS AND TUTORS IN PART-TIME SERVICE		
Robert Hales	1602	singer
Cormack MacDermott	Oct. 1605 - May 1612	Irish harp
John Lanier	July 1605 - Dec. 1610	tutor
Innocent Lanier	Feb. 1607 - Oct. 1609	tutor
John Coprario	Apr. 1603 - May 1612	viol/tutor
Joseph Sherley	Oct. 1609 - Oct. 1610	viol/tutor
Thomas Robinson		cittern
APPRENTICES		
Daniel, formerly Lord Burgh's apprentice	Feb. 1596 -?	instrumentalist
Henry Phillips	Dec. 1598 -?	?
Nicholas Lanier	July 1605 - Oct. 1607	singer/lute/viol/flute
George Mason	Feb. 1607 - Aug. 1608	singer/viol/lute
Christian Crusse	Jan. 1608 - Dec. 1610	viol/?singer
Simon (?Ives)	Oct. 1608 - Oct. 1609	singer/viol/lute
UNCERTAIN		
Antony Holborne	1599 - 1602	?
Charles Tessier		?
Sir Richard Champernown's boy	requested Aug. 1595	singer
Thomas Lord Burgh's 3 boys	offered in 1596	instrumentalists and singers, including one treble and one high mean
Antony Holborne's son	offered in 1606	?

was willing to continue in the same role until the completion of his son's indenture so that 'it wilbe no prejudice to your Lordshippes service'. However, the following year the post was given to someone else and it was not until 1616 that Nicholas joined the King's Musick. Likewise, Cecil's keyboard player, William Frost, sued for the vacant post of virginal teacher to Princess Elizabeth but the place was filled by one of Prince Henry's musicians, the composer and virginalist John Bull. Cecil was undoubtedly in a position to influence both appointments, but may have preferred his own interests above those of his servants.

The consort was expected to entertain Cecil and his guests in both the public (the great hall) and private spaces (the great chamber, the withdrawing chamber and the chapel) within his various residences – Salisbury House on the Strand in London and Theobalds and Hatfield in Hertfordshire – and in his chambers at Whitehall Palace. Between 1607 and 1609 the consort also took part in the royal entertainments staged by Cecil to flatter the Crown and to impress his contemporaries. In the printed edition of *The Genius*, performed at Theobalds on 22 May 1607 to mark the formal transfer of Cecil's country seat to Anne of Denmark in exchange for Hatfield, the playwright Ben Jonson recorded that the concluding song 'O blessed change' was prefaced with 'rare and choise Musique' and the song itself was 'deliver'd by an excellent voice'.

According to the early seventeenth-century treatise 'Some rules and orders for the government of the house of an Earle', household musicians were also required to teach their master's children to sing and to play on a variety of instruments, including the bass viol, lute and virginal. Cecil's daughter Frances, who was a skilled virginalist, was probably tutored by Frost while her brother, William Lord Cranborne, studied on the bass viol both at home and at St John's College, Cambridge, with Nicholas Lanier.

The instrument collection stored at Salisbury House and in Cecil's Hertfordshire mansions comprised at least four virginals; five organs, including three 'great wind instruments' and two portative organs (from the Latin

The great organ purchased from John Haan, a Dutch merchant, in 1608, standing in the Armoury at Hatfield.

verb *portare* meaning 'to carry'); an Irish or wire-string harp; a bass violin or cello; and several lutes and viols. Additional instruments would have been provided by the musicians themselves or borrowed from other patrons as occasion demanded. For example, Sir Fulke Greville, who was keen to ingratiate himself with the Secretary of State, thanked Cecil in May 1612 for returning an instrument which he described as 'honoured by his Lordship's use of it'.

All that remains today of the instrument collection is

A panel from the organ painted in the grotesque style, adapted from a plate published in Newes Gradesca Büchlein *(Augsburg, 1607).*

Buckett, responsible for painting much of the interior at Hatfield. In July 1611 the organ maker Thomas Dallam, who took care of the organs in the royal palaces and was employed to tune and repair Cecil's keyboard instruments for an annual fee of £2, set up the organ in the great chamber in the east range at Hatfield where it was used to accompany chamber music.

We know from a library catalogue compiled several months after Cecil's death that the musicians had access to 'Diverse Bookes of musicke and songes', the contents of which are not recorded. The surviving household accounts are equally uninformative, listing only 'three great violl bookes with gilt Covers' purchased by Nicholas Lanier in December 1607. At the very least the collection must have included presentation copies of the works dedicated to Cecil: Thomas Morley's *The First Booke of Balletts* (London, 1595), Robert Jones, *The First Set of Madrigals of 3, 4, 5, 6, 7 and 8 Parts* (London, 1607) and John Dowland's translation of the sixteenth-century German musical treatise *Andreas Ornithoparcus his Micrologus* (London, 1609). In all probability Cecil also received a copy of Thomas Robinson's *New Citharen Lessons* (London, 1609), dedicated to Lord Cranborne and written for the popular wire-strung cittern. In the dedicatory epistle Robinson recalls the 'comfortable liberalitie' of Cecil's patronage and the volume opens with a pair of dances (a pavan and galliard) in celebration of Cecil's recent appointment as Lord Treasurer. Despite the lack of evidence we can still draw some conclusions about the music Cecil enjoyed.

Cecil was passionate about vocal music, though what was actually sung is more difficult to determine. Given that his cultural sympathies lay south of the Alps, it is reasonable to suppose that he shared the Italianate musical taste of many of his contemporaries, including his friend, the 7th Earl of Shrewsbury, dedicatee of *Musica Transalpina* (1588), England's first printed anthology of translated Italian madrigals. Thomas Morley, who founded the English madrigal school, was generously rewarded by Cecil in 1595 for his dedication of *The First Booke of Balletts*, issued in parallel English and Italian editions, possibly with a view to selling the

the large domestic organ which stands at the west end of the Armoury at Hatfield. Possibly built in northern Europe, the organ was one of several sumptuous goods acquired in November 1608 at a cost of £1060 from John Haan, a Dutch merchant. The price of the instrument is not specified, but in all probability Cecil paid a considerable sum of money for it. (Domestic organs around this time generally cost less than £100). The ornately decorated Jacobean case which houses a much later instrument is the work of the artist Rowland

The cantus part of 'Now is the month of Maying' from the English version of Thomas Morley's The First Booke of Balletts *(London, 1595), no. 3.*

publication on the Continent. The ballet, which is the simplest form of Italian music naturalised by Morley, consists of a strophic setting with a 'fa la' refrain. 'Now is the month of Maying' is probably the best known piece from the collection. Morley's publication is based on Giovanni Gastoldi's popular 1591 Venetian print *Balletti a Cinque Voci*. Both sets contain twenty-one pieces, of which fifteen are ballets; eight of Gastoldi's poems are used in the Italian edition of Morley's print; and both composers close their publication with a dia-

logue for double chorus, found in several Italian prints of the time.

As for his taste in instrumental music, Cecil kept abreast of the latest developments through his patronage of the leading exponents in the field. Between about 1603 and 1612 he employed five viol players on a full-time or part-time basis: Sherley, Oxford, Nicholas Lanier, Crusse and Coprario (not an Italian by birth, as his surname would suggest, but plain John Cooper who had 'affected an Itallian termination' in order to gain patronage). One of the major advances in Jacobean viol consort music was the new multi-sectional fantasy (a musical composition in which rapid fugal sections alternate with slow moving passages) that evolved from the five-part polyphonic Italian madrigal. The earliest examples, modelled on existing vocal compositions, soon gave way to original fantasias influenced by the madrigal style. Crucial to this development were the five-part works of Coprario, composed during Cecil's lifetime.

Playing on the viol lyra-way, using French lute tablature instead of staff notation in a variety of tunings, rapidly grew in popularity during the first two decades of the seventeenth century. Tablature is a form of notation used for fretted string instruments like the viol and lute, or the guitar today. The French system uses a six-line grid in which the top line represents the highest string with letters indicating the frets (a for open string, b for first fret, and so on). Note values are placed above the grid to indicate the rhythm.

Cecil was a key patron in the early history of the technique, and two of his musicians, Sherley and Coprario, were among the handful of composers who experimented with the lyra style. The chest of viols at Salisbury House included a lyra, a purpose-built instrument, smaller than the standard consort bass, designed to facilitate chordal playing, an inherent feature of the genre. *Poeticall Musicke* (1607), the second of Tobias Hume's pioneering collections in the lyra style, contains a piece in honour of Cecil, 'Sweet musicke' or 'The Earle of Salisburies fauoret/delight'.

Praised by Cecil's cousin, Sir Francis Bacon, for its melting and prolonged sound, the Irish wire-strung harp appealed to a number of English musical patrons. In 1597 Cecil received a harp from the Irish peeress Eleanor, Countess of Desmond, in the hope of currying favour, and from around February 1603 he maintained the Irish harpist Cormack MacDermott. The traditional use of the harp to accompany improvised epic song had died out in court circles earlier in the sixteenth century, but MacDermott developed a new repertory for the instrument in which polyphonic art music was scored both for the solo harp and in consort with other instruments.

Cecil shared Bacon's curiosity for acoustical experiment. In or around December 1607 he acquired a viol with sympathetic strings that ran parallel to the playing strings along the length of the belly and vibrated when the instrument was bowed. This viol had been invented by Arthur Gregory, a client of the Cecil family since the 1580s, and made by the royal musician George Gill, who later applied for the monopoly, albeit unsuccessfully, to make string instruments with 'an addicion of wyer stringes'. Gregory's invention received a mixed response. Bacon, for instance regarded the device 'to be of no use, because the upper *Strings*, which are stopped in great variety, cannot maintain a *Diapason* [octave] or *Unison*, with the Lower, which are never stopped.'

The presence of a claviorganum among the keyboard instruments at Salisbury House is another example of Cecil's interest in acoustics. Described as 'a great Harpesicall wynd Instrum't with virginall in it', the instrument was probably a double or triple strung full-size harpsichord incorporating a positive organ, similar to the claviorganum on display in the British Galleries in the Victoria and Albert Museum, made in London in 1579 by the Dutch craftsman Lodewijk Theeuwes. The combined sound of plucked strings and blown pipes was of minority appeal, though it is interesting that Cecil's household chaplain, George Montaigne, also owned such an instrument.

There can be little doubt that Cecil enjoyed music. He was a skilful auditor and used his knowledge of the art to maintain a consort of some of the best singers and instrumentalists of the late Elizabethan and early Jacobean periods. Moreover, Cecil was aware of the latest musical trends, from the fashionable Italianate compositions of Morley and the other English madrigalists to the more esoteric developments in the field of instrumental music, and provided a favourable environment in which composers like Coprario and McDermott were able to experiment with the latest musical styles.

This chapter is based predominantly on two earlier publications by the author, 'The Musical Patronage of Robert Cecil, First Earl of Salisbury (1563–1612)', *Journal of the Royal Musical Association*, 116/1 (1991), pp 24–40 and "Musique which pleaseth myne eare': Robert Cecil's Musical Patronage' in *Patronage, Culture and Power: the Early Cecils, 1558–1612*, edited by Pauline Croft (Yale University Press, London and New Haven, 2002), pp 139–158.

The Chapel

DOUGLAS SLATER

Douglas Slater began his working life as a Clerk in the House of Lords, moonlighting as deputy theatre critic for the Daily Mail. *Since the mid-1990s he has been a freelance adviser on a range of topics from constitutional reform to arts policy.*

ROBERT CECIL'S new house at Hatfield had a number of novel features. Not the least was the chapel he put at its heart. It may be slightly off-centre – like the human heart – but it is impossible to get from the west side to the rest of the house on either of the principal floors without passing by or through it.

As Lord David Cecil pointed out in *The Cecils of Hatfield House* forty years ago, chapels in country houses are not so unusual, but the one at Hatfield is different from the usual run. He remarked that this was still a sacred place, and it remains so today. The prayer books piled at the ends of the pews have the look of being used because they are. Morning Prayer is said here every day, and the Litany on Friday, and Holy Communion is celebrated on Sunday. It is perhaps one of the few places left in England where one can reliably still hear the service of Morning Prayer as it is set out in the Book of Common Prayer, with nothing added and nothing left out, although the shorter options are mostly adopted. Lady Salisbury has timed it at 13 minutes – one must know to plan breakfast – and it is a daily 13 minutes that Robert Cecil would find familiar.

William Cecil, Robert's father, would have known Thomas Cranmer, the Archbishop of Canterbury who compiled the classic 'three-legged stool' of the Anglican liturgy – Morning Prayer, Evening Prayer and Holy

OPPOSITE *A rare survival: the east window of the Chapel still contains brightly-coloured painted glass dating from 1609–10.*

Communion – out of the daily cycle of Latin services in the Roman Catholic breviary. Cranmer's was an inspired act of creative editing. It is central to the Anglican establishment, poised between Roman Catholicism and Protestantism, capable of being described as 'reformed but not Protestant' for those whose religious beliefs take them that way, leaving Anglicanism with its own claim to the Apostolic Succession. It was a key element of the religious settlement that first Elizabeth I and William Cecil, and then James I and Robert Cecil, sought to enforce. Cranmer translated the Roman Catholic Latin into an English of clarity and vigour, creating a liturgy in which nothing was too dogmatic – so that most ordinary people could go along with it – while leaving very little to the potential perversity of the individual conscience. His political aim was to isolate the extremes: Thomas Cranmer, rather than Thomas More, was truly the Man For All Seasons.

Nowadays it is hard to praise the Book of Common Prayer without seeming to disparage newer liturgies in use, and this is no place to stumble into the passionate rows that liturgy can still provoke. At least no-one is now martyred over an order of service. Inshallah. Still, it seems ungenerous not to notice what an extraordinary job Thomas Cranmer – who was martyred – made of his cut-and-paste job. For the matchless language of those 13 minutes covers our human concerns pretty well. Day by day, there is little in the *Today* programme that they do not reflect. The daily observance in the Chapel is not

The carved woodwork in the lower chapel dates from the restoration by the 3rd Marquess of Salisbury in 1869.

the least of the continuity that Hatfield represents.

If that robust continuity is what Robert Cecil hoped for, he did not create it by making his Chapel something modest or unremarkable. For its date, the Chapel is an extraordinarily lavishly decorated space, worthy of comparison with any chapel on the continent of Europe, where mannerism was developing with the encouragement of the Counter-Reformation Roman Catholic Church into the baroque. Robert Cecil, with his love of the arts and of display, was running the strong risk of Puritan disapproval, and accusations of crypto-popery.

His own religious views were as subtle as the rest of his thought, but as Pauline Croft has argued convincingly those views seem to have developed considerably from the time of his early education in his father's house and at Cambridge, from what she describes as 'orthodox Elizabethan Protestantism' to a more complex position in line with the trends that led to Laudianism, and the religious conflicts of the seventeenth century. She describes him as the first great patron of the emerging high church party, and his Chapel reflects that.

Perhaps he felt he could afford to run the risk of accusations of crypto-popery. He had acquiesced to an extent usually alien to his personality in the savagery that had been visited on the Gunpowder Plotters: popery was not now practical politics, and Robert Cecil was nothing if not a practical politician. He remained at pains to restrain James's intellectualized leaning towards formal toleration. It could only lead to trouble.

It was the Puritans at the opposite end of the religious spectrum who were more of a problem, and Cecil had seen them effectively snubbed by the King in the Authorised Version of the Bible prepared following the Hampton Court Conference of 1604. The Puritans had asked James for a new translation of the Bible, and he had given it to them whilst giving nothing else. He had then ensured that the new Bible bore few traces of the Geneva Bible that he found so offensive to his views on kingship.

The Authorised Version of the Bible – the King James Bible – was being prepared at exactly the same time as the new house at Hatfield was being built. As Adam Nicolson among others has remarked, this makes them twins: the one in stone and brick and wood and paint, the other in words. This gives Robert Cecil's Chapel its special significance. What is more, Hatfield still houses the nearest thing that exists to the first copy of the King James Bible, the one that Cecil claimed from the King's printer as was his right as a Privy Councellor, and had bound in a binding of sumptuous richness. So it might be said without being too fanciful that at Hatfield we come as near to the heart of the Anglican settlement as it is possible to come: spirituality and the secular need for stability held in a careful political tension, the state respectful of God and His church but in no danger of giving too much power to divines of any persuasion, glorious yet domestic.

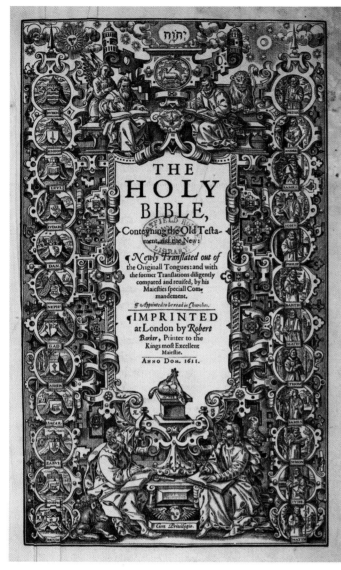

Title-page of Robert Cecil's copy of the King James Bible, 1611.

in England for seventy years. It is still there, a cycle of sermons in glass, twelve panels illustrating different scenes from the Old Testament, each by a reference at the bottom of the picture linking it to the New Testament event or text that seventeenth century scholarship regarded as its counterpart. And scholarship it was. This is not the Bible in English: the footnotes are still in scholars' Latin.

Most of the panels seem to be by a Flemish artist, Martin van Bentheim, but one at least – that of Solomon and the Queen of Sheba – is by a Frenchman, Louis Dauphin. Its inscription is in French rather than Latin. The story of Jonah is by one Richard Butler 'of Southwark', who may have been English or have come from the Low Countries and anglicized his name. The whole window works together with a characteristically Jacobean heterodoxy. Its compelling charm lies in its cheerful artistic licence: Pharaoh's palace is a French brick chateau, Delilah betrays Samson in a room of Roman marbled grandeur (the hussy), and Naaman's camel patiently waits on the banks of the river Jordan, anatomically somewhat strange but wearing a look of authentic aristocratic disdain.

It was not just the stained glass that made the Chapel splendid and unusual. Robert Cecil commissioned Rowland Buckett both to paint religious pictures and to decorate and gild the walls and gallery. Buckett was the son of a German immigrant. He is first heard of in Istanbul in 1599, painting a portrait of Elizabeth I for the Sultan's wife, and decorating an organ to be a gift to the Sultan (although it never seems to have reached him). That was presumably a government commission for diplomatic purposes, which may explain how he came to Robert Cecil's attention. No-one would accuse Buckett of being a great painter, but he was a perfectly competent one. One also suspects that he was rather likeable. Admittedly, painters did not enjoy any great status in England at that time – this was before Rubens came to England as both ambassador and artist, and was knighted – but Buckett seems to have been happy to turn his hand to anything, indoors or out. He enjoyed a happy relationship both with Robert Cecil and his son,

If the Chapel is remarkable now, it must have provoked something like shock in those who first saw it four hundred years ago. They were used to private chapels with little or no ornament. Ornament had gone during the reign of Edward VI when Cranmer had prepared his Prayer Book. At Hatfield, Robert Cecil installed the first new stained glass window to be seen

The betrayal of Samson by Delilah in one of the stained glass panels.

William. It is good to report that he was well rewarded over many years, including with the lease of a house in St Martin's Lane. Among other pictures for the Chapel he painted an Annunciation, and an Annunciation to the Shepherds, as well as the figures in grisaille around the window, and some particularly charming cherubs around the gallery. All are still in place.

So the claim can tentatively be made: with its elaborate decoration, Robert Cecil's Chapel at Hatfield architecturally marks the beginning of the high church tendency in the Church of England, when the Reformation began to seem sufficiently well established to permit of being embellished. The young William Laud was a protégé of Cecil, although as events were to show he lacked his patron's sure sense of knowing how far he could go. He paid with his archepiscopal head.

The Civil War was to mark the catastrophic breakdown of the Elizabethan religious settlement that William and Robert Cecil fought to maintain. In its early years Robert's son, the 2nd Earl, prudently took down the stained glass and put it into storage, as a precaution, even though he was an adherent of Parliament rather than the King. It is in fact almost a miracle that as much of Robert Cecil's original decoration has survived as has.

The preservation of the Chapel in the fire of 1835 that destroyed the rest of the west wing, and the Dowager 1st Marchioness with it, seemed to contemporaries a miracle also. In fact – although who is to say that miracles are not facts? – there were lead water tanks in the roof just short of the Chapel which were melted by the flames, thus effectively dowsing them. In any event, the Chapel was saved.

After 1868, another Robert, the 3rd Marquess, re-ordered and re-decorated the ground floor of the Chapel in line with his own religious convictions. Those convictions were strong, like most of his views, but also subtle and paradoxical, and more than somewhat enigmatic. He was the Salisbury who became Prime Minister. He was also a Fellow of All Souls. He would have looked his two great predecessors the Lords Treasurer in the eye, if not seen eye to eye with them: it would be a rash

The Annunciation, painted by Rowland Buckett in 1611.

top of his formidable bent. His biographer, Andrew Roberts, sums it up neatly enough: 'If a tolerant High Anglican fundamentalism is not doubly oxymoronic, it defines Cecil's lifelong faith'. And though he professed to be a complete Philistine, he imported Bolognese marble to enrich the sanctuary, hung the walls of the Chapel with pictures, and furnished it with an ornate organ, carved pews and an elegant marble font. The Chapel today is essentially as it was when he died in 1903.

It was his daughter-in-law Violet Maxse who was famously welcomed to Hatfield by him as 'to Gaza, the capital of Philistia', as is mentioned elsewhere by the present Lord Salisbury. She must have recalled that in 1934 when as Viscountess Milner she gave to the Chapel the Cruxifixion now attributed to Adrian Isenbrandt (although she bought it at auction as being by Rogier van der Weyden) in memory of her first husband Lord Edward, and their son George who was killed in the First World War.

Prime Minister Salisbury would – surely? – have approved of Evensong being the climax of the weekend to celebrate Hatfield's quatercentenary; Evening Prayer would have been said in his day in any event, and his incorporation of an organ into his reordering of the Chapel argues for music being acceptable, indifferent though he was to music as to all the other arts. That there is to be a new commission by our greatest contemporary composer of religious music – James MacMillan – could be scarcely more appropriate, for Salisbury appointed the first Roman Catholic Cabinet Minister since the reign of James II. And the text for the new anthem must pass muster: Psalm 127, 'Except the Lord build the house, they labour in vain that build it', in the King James Bible's version, in honour of its quatercentenary.

And the congregation will sit as they sat in his day, and as they always sit in the Chapel at Hatfield: men to the left side facing the altar, women on the right. For the Chapel remains as Lord David described it, 'a sacred place set apart'.

person who would say categorically where he would agree or disagree with anyone. He was of the generation that had grown up with Tractarianism in all its Victorian piety, but also with the Victorian revolution in science, in which he took a great interest. When he was a teenager he had had a compelling religious experience that remained with him throughout his life. He never said what it was, but it gave him an absolute faith overriding any mundane question of why the world was or is as it was or is. He was a man of action who doubted whether it did any good, but acted anyway, and to the

The Gardens at Hatfield

HANNAH SALISBURY

W<small>E ARE</small> all familiar with the signposts 'Hatfield and the North'. It was the first staging post on the way out of London, and in 1850 when the railway came, it was not surprising that Hatfield should be the first stop. The Salisburys had been used to travelling to London from the south side, taking the 'Duke's Ride' through the Park straight to the Great North Road. The train was now the ideal way of going to London and in 1877 a viaduct was built giving access to the station; gradually the focus of the House turned to face the station and the north, and the House, surrounded by parkland and ancient oak trees, presented a sterner aspect when approached from this side.

In 1948 the House was opened to the public. The tarmac forecourt was made ready for cars, buses and camper vans. Unsurprisingly a visitor's first glimpse of this great Jacobean house was disappointing. My husband's dream had always been to get rid of the tarmac, commission a great centre piece and surround it with grass. Planning permission had to be obtained as well as alternative parking for visitors arranged, and in 2011 the car park was finally moved west, behind the Old Palace. At the time of writing, conscious of the enormous upheaval mess and expense that removing tarmac entails (550 lorry loads) we have decided to approach the landscaping of the North Front in several bites. Firstly the grass circle will be laid out, which will immediately uplift and enhance this space. Then, in the autumn of 2011, more tarmac will be removed to

Lady Salisbury and Alan Titchmarsh, the television presenter and writer, in the garden at Hatfield House.

accommodate two double rows of limes on both the east and west sides which will, in time, be pleached to complement the proportions of the House as well as the circle. The dream will come true when a beautiful fountain becomes a reality. Every project at Hatfield is so huge that on the grounds of expense alone, the works have to be phased and budgeted for accordingly.

Generations of Cecils since the time of Robert Cecil have planned and planted, altered and added, removed and replaced, and the tradition continues. Ideas both for inside the house as well as in the garden are chewed over, much discussed and quite often become a reality. My intention is to write about the garden but there is no part of the garden which does not have the House in the background, or vice versa. Our predecessors through the centuries achieved the most harmonious relationship between the two.

Hatfield House from the air, showing the car park with buses parked on the North Front.

Architectural drawing showing plans for the North Front.

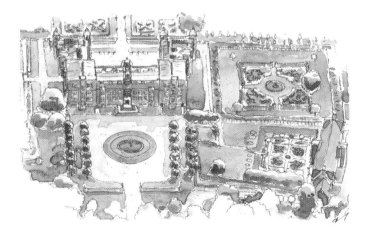

The Knot Garden and Old Palace.

The garden at Hatfield was as much of a passion for Robert Cecil as the building of the house. It is hard to believe that as chief minister to James I he had time to be involved in the planning of both.

In 1607 Robert acquired the old manor house of Hatfield but it was old fashioned and not a suitable building to satisfy his dynastic aspirations; the old Tudor Palace had belonged to the Bishop of Ely until the Dissolution and was where both Mary and then Elizabeth spent many years out of sight and away from the court. Robert demolished three sides of the Old Palace, leaving the great hall with its magnificent roof timbers

which we see today. Adjacent, but now with more space between, the new house was built in five years, and was more or less finished by 1611.

Throughout those years, together with men whose taste he admired, he worked on a series of designs and 'plots', using them, discarding them, changing his mind, constantly adapting and improving until he achieved what he wanted. 'Many plots' were designed in 1607 by Mountain Jennings who had been Robert Cecil's gardener at Theobalds (a magnificent house left to him by Burghley and subsequently exchanged for Hatfield) and Robert Lyminge who was paid for surveying and

Carved figure of a gardener holding a rake on the Grand Staircase said to be John Tradescant.

plotting of 'Hattfeld Howses' the same year. Salomon de Caus was employed to design the East Garden. The most adventurous gardener of his day, he was full of ideas including solar-powered machines which produced music, and an original hydraulic system to operate the fountains in the East Garden. John Tradescant the Elder was sent abroad in search of rare and beautiful plants and returned with gillyflowers, pomegranates, jonquils, tulips, roses and the famous double anemone.

By April 1612 Tradescant was back at Hatfield, where he submitted another bill for 'seedes and other necessaryes bought for the kitchen garden'. Costing forty shillings and a penny, his purchases were '24 earthen panns' and 'two water tubbs' for melons, as well as onion, spinach, sweet marjoram, bugloss, borage and marigold seed. The bills also include two garden rakes, two pairs of shears and the cost of replacing the handles on three mattocks. Twelve bundles of small hazels 'to mend the hedges in the gardens' were also noted, as well as the inevitable 'dunge' – five loads this time.

With his death in 1612 at the age of 49, Robert Cecil was unable to enjoy the fruits of his great creation; all the planning and anticipation was thwarted as he travelled unsuccessfully in search of a cure for his galloping cancer. His son William continued to employ Tradescant for a short time but the rare pomegranates and exotics

The double anemone Anemone pluchée, painted by Jean-Baptiste Monnoyer (1636–1699) at Hatfield.

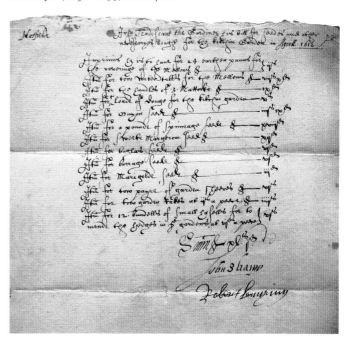

Bill submitted by John Tradescant 'for seeds & divers other necessaries', including two pairs of garden shears and '24 earthen pans for covering mellons,' April 1612 (Bills 69).

died from lack of care and the 'Vignerons' left, with the vines succumbing to the mini Ice Age in the second quarter of the seventeenth century.

John Evelyn in 1643 wrote, 'I went to see my Lord Salisbury's Palace at Hatfield where the most considerable rarity besides the house (inferior to few in England for its architecture) was the garden and vineyard rarely well watered and planted.' In July 1661 it was Pepys' turn, writing in his diary, 'So by degrees, till I come to Hatfield before twelve oclock, & walked all alone to the Vineyard, which is now a very beautiful place again; & coming back I met with Mr Looker, my Lords gardener who showed me the house, the chapel with brave pictures, & above all, the gardens, such as I never saw in all my life, nor so good flowers, nor so great gooseburys, as big as nutmegs.' Six years later, on a second visit, he wrote, 'Then we to our inn & there dined very well & mighty merry; & walked out into the Park through the fine walk of trees, & to the Vineyard, & there shewed them that, which is in good order, & indeed a place of great delight; which, together with our fine walk through the park, was of as much pleasure as could be desired in the world for country pleasure & good air.'

But the gardens declined steadily, reaching a nadir in the middle of the eighteenth century, when the 6th Earl of Salisbury lived as a recluse at Quickswood, a property near Baldock. Nothing at Hatfield, either in the house or in the garden was created, adapted or maintained. Referring to those days, Lady Gwendolen Cecil, younger daughter of Prime Minister Salisbury wrote 'the general mediocrity of intelligence the family displayed was only varied by instances of quite exceptional stupidity.'

The brave, high-spirited and pleasure-loving Emily Mary, the 1st Marchioness, brought Hatfield back from its long hibernation. She devoted much of her time to hunting. The garden in the prevailing fashion of the day was largely swept away, with the park conveniently coming up to the walls of the House from where she could dismount from her horse.

Though no gardener, Emily Mary started her 'experi-

An illustration from The Third Tour of Dr. Syntax *of the First Marchioness riding in the Park, 1821.*

mental ground' in 1795. She and her bailiff Mr Stephenson 'experimented with the most unusual crops. She fed cabbage to cows and sometimes carrots. Parsnips were used to fatten oxen and bullocks and red beet for cattle food.' In his *General View of the Agriculture of the County of Hertfordshire* in 1804, Arthur Young gave a vivid description of the 'ground':

The experimental-ground of the Marchioness of Salisbury was one of the most interesting spectacles which I saw in Hertfordshire. It is a field of 17 acres, thoroughly well fenced, surrounded with a margin of grass, and with two cross-walks, for the pleasing convenience of viewing the crops: they are well worth viewing, and do no slight honour to the talents of the cultivator.

In 1795 the experimental ground was prepared.

In 1796. This year it produced red beets, mangel worzel, parsnips, carrots and cabbages.

In 1797. Half various sorts of cabbages, and half different roots.

In 1798. Where the cabbages had been last year, roots were grown, and after the roots of last year, cabbages. The cleanness of the crops, their flourishing luxuriance, and the general aspect of the whole, are truly pleasing. I could not, however, but regret that a register had not been kept of every crop, the expense, produce, and consumption per acre; this field would then not have yielded pleasure only, but an ample harvest of agricultural knowledge; and, with a few variations easy to have devised, would have produced a fund of important conclusions.

In 1835, by then a venerable old Dowager, poor Emily Mary was engulfed in the flames that destroyed the West Wing of the house. The young Charles Dickens writing for the *Morning Chronicle* hurried down from London to report on the catastrophe. He was later to recycle the fire in *Oliver Twist*, making Bill Sikes a spectator to the 'half dressed figures tearing to and fro, some endeavouring to drag the frightened horses from the stables, others driving the cattle from the yard and outhouses, and others coming laden from the burning pile, amidst a shower of falling sparks and the tumbling down of red-hot beams.'

It was Emily Mary's son, the 2nd Marquess, who began the great task of not only rebuilding the West Wing but also restoring the gardens to how he thought they had originally been. He made terraces on both the east and west sides of the House; he laid out new parterres and planted a maze at the bottom of the East Garden where his ancestor Robert had dreamt of fountains in the shapes of seahorses, canals and water spouting out of mermaids. He was the first Salisbury since his ancestor

Larry Laird clipping the maze.

Robert, to create as well as restore, and it is to him that we look, with both admiration and gratitude.

Larry Laird, a Liverpudlian by birth, came to Hatfield in the 1960s and his job was to clip all the hedges, the topiary, the knot gardens, the East Garden and beech hedges and the maze. He used traditional clipping shears attached to a tractor whose engine brought the power through a long cable to where he was working. In the maze he painstakingly clipped along each of the alleys, entered each of the dead ends, and, in the middle, resting on top of a yew plinth, he created two recumbent lions, one guarding the north entrance and the other the south. Until his retirement last year, the maze was clipped every September, and it was always his last job before going on holiday. Larry had an expert eye which has never been bettered. He was an artist,

The West Wing after the fire of November 27th 1835.

critically observing his work from every angle and compensating when the ground levels altered – sometimes by several feet – so that the hedges always appeared straight. Sadly this work is now contracted out.

Describing a garden and what grows in it can be risky; favourite shrubs might not survive the winter; they may outgrow their usefulness, become diseased, fall out of favour and be grubbed up; they may be moved to a sunnier spot or where there is better drainage. Anything can happen, as was evident when I recently visited a beautiful garden in Yorkshire. The owner had drawn out an elaborate and detailed map of her borders, what they contained and where they were planted. It was impressive, beautifully illustrated, and altogether a magnificent effort, but in very few instances did the name of the plant on the plan coincide with what was in the ground. I suspect that she had forgotten how much work she had done to improve this glorious border. This is how gardens evolve, constantly changing, constantly improving, and always waiting for next year when it will be approaching perfection.

I should, nevertheless, like to risk a short description of the garden as it has evolved over the last hundred years, the designs and improvements that have been made by the various incumbents, and finally to take you on a walk through the Shrubbery. We are making a serious effort to label the shrubs and trees, as well as the roses and plants. Quite often these labels prove to be irresistible to the light-fingered visitor. Perhaps they forgot to bring a pencil?

All four sides of the house now have a garden. The North Front which I have already described is the side to a house which normally remains more private, and where you might expect to see washing lines, coal sheds, oil tanks, dustbins, logs, cars and even a garage. Here, secret recesses exist: logs are delivered down a shute into the basement, the heating plant is modern and takes up two basement rooms and resembles a ship's engine room, clean, and shining brightly, with yards of new thickly-lagged pipes all of which are controlled by efficient computers. Most of the rubbish is recycled, and the rest is kept below the steps and unseen. The milk,

the letters and the laundry are delivered to the office door on the West Terrace. The old kitchen, to the west of the front door and now part of the house open to visitors, has recently been restored recalling Queen Victoria's visit in 1846. This kitchen was used when the house was built; subsequently kitchens have moved around to suit the needs of the time. The kitchen that we made in 2006 facing east is a great delight: it is the house's first non-subterranean kitchen and is the centre from where everything originates: messages arrive, family, dogs and friends congregate, babies are fed, and dogs loiter hopefully. And the most delicious meals are created.

Below the terrace is the East Garden, designed by my husband's grandparents. Laid out symmetrically are 16 square box-edged beds with topiarized middles and planted with mixed herbaceous, roses, peonies, irises and many different salvias. On either side are 'hot' borders which remain bright and cheerful until the first frost. Again, the proportions of this garden are sympathetic to the strangely cobbled-together east façade and can be seen from the first floor rooms. Building on these bones, my mother-in-law, the present Dowager, did much to improve this garden, adding the topiary to the centre of each of the beds, as well as two avenues of standard Ilex trees running down on either side, thus

The Dowager Marchioness of Salisbury, who has been instrumental in helping redesign the gardens.

The East Garden from the East Terrace.

creating much needed height and variations in textured greens. She replaced the central avenue of Irish Yews with the Common Yew and introduced classical statues looking out over the garden from the terrace. Below is the maze and further down still, the New Pond, and the site where Robert Cecil had hoped to realize his great water parterre. The lake is still referred to as the 'New Pond' although it was created when the house was built. On the northern corner, there is an Elizabethan brick doorway which was brought from Hatfield Woodhall, a small manor house in the parish. The boathouse is below.

On a bank on the east side of the maze, *Buddleja davidii* 'Black Knight', 'Locchinch', 'Blue Profusion', and 'Dartmoor' are planted to attract butterflies and quite recently, spotted and marsh orchids began to appear in the long grass opposite. Mature as well as

newly-planted trees form a backdrop to the water and well-deserved prominence is given to the old veteran oaks and hornbeams. *Acer griseum, Malus Transitoria, Cercidiphyllum, Malus* 'Joseph Rock' and *Prunus serrula* are among the many young trees that have recently been planted. There is a very fine fiery red *Hamamelis* 'Feuezanber' behind which is a path planted with a collection of specie roses.

On leaving the East Garden you pass through the new 'potager' created by my mother-in-law. She did so for practical as well as aesthetic reasons, since the original massive walled kitchen garden lies half a mile away, beyond the shrubbery. On your right is where I keep my assorted collection of bantams and large fowl: Silkies, Silver Lace and Barred Wyandottes, Millefleur citron-booted Sablefoot, Millefleur Pekins, Sebrights, Buff

The West Garden with its octagonal fountain in the centre.

Orpingtons and Marans and a single blue egg-laying Cream Legbar. The occasional depredations of the dreaded urban fox cause the cast to change, and though miserable and furious, I return to the Livestock Market and sometimes manage to do a bit of swapping with fellow poultry enthusiasts.

Dominating the West Garden is the ancient Lime Walk, pleached and encircling the garden created by Lady Gwendolen Cecil, the younger daughter of Prime Minister Salisbury. She designed a waving inner yew hedge enclosing a large parterre which remains with its original layout still intact. The planting of course has changed, as tastes have changed. It is still labour-intensive: planting and replacing, pruning, and cutting back takes time and the flowering season is thus extended into the autumn. Large gardens have had to invest in labour-saving machinery and Hatfield is no exception. Where there were 40 gardeners in 1914, 36 gardeners in 1930, 26 in 1939 and 13 in 1958, now, we manage on five. Led by Alistair Gunn, a dedicated and knowledgeable plantsman, and his hard-working and enthusiastic team, Simon the foreman gardener, Peter, Mat and Tom.

Some of the Garden staff in 1924.

The Garden team in 2011 headed by Alastair Gunn in the centre.

At the steps leading away from the Lime Walk, quince trees and mounds of the creamy-white *pittisporum* 'Irene Patterson' repeat the length of a blue and white border filled with *Iris pallida var. pallida*, rare *Buddleja colvilei, Buddleja lindleyana*, lupins, Nepeta, lavenders and *Clematis* 'Alba Luxuriens'.

Below the West Garden is the sundial garden. The newly-installed 'Hatfield Longitude Dial' by William Andrewes commemorates the 400th anniversary of the building of Hatfield House. The shapes, colours and scale of the plants surrounding the armillary sphere should not compete with a model of the heavens used for teaching astronomy in the early seventeenth century.

In front of the holly hedge, the raised beds contain old-fashioned and shrub roses which are under-planted with dianthus. On either side of the sundial, my mother-in-law planted a box tunnel running the length of this enclosed garden. Its intersecting alleys gives it an architectural quality.

From the sundial and the long blue and white border you pass through the wrought iron gates into the Shrubbery or wilderness garden. Criss-crossing the whole of the seven acres of this wild garden are grass paths on

LEFT *An Elizabethan brick doorway which was brought from Hatfield Woodhall, a small manor house in the parish.*

BELOW *The West Garden borders, laid out by Lady Gwendolen Cecil with their curved yew hedges.*

OPPOSITE *A new blue and white border from the south with the Old Palace in the background.*

each side of which we leave the grass uncut until later in the year, so that the wild flowers can flourish and set their seed. First planted in the early nineteenth century, it still contains several examples of the early hybrids of *Rhododendron Arboreum*. Also predating the Victorian shrubbery are the grand old oaks, beech, sequoias, yew and holly, which provide shade and shape to this long strip running alongside the Deer Park and away from the house. When the rhododendrons were planted, a large quantity of peat was imported to make special beds in which these, as well as other acid-loving plants were established. Sadly the ancient Himalayan species became unfashionable in the twentieth century, and many of them were grubbed up.

Walking south through a 'quincunx' of young limes with the Holly Walk on your right, you come to a stone urn surrounded by *Quercus suber*, the cork oak. From

The early hybrid, Rhododendron Arboreum.

there can be seen *Philadelphus coronarius*, *Betula utilis var. jacquemontii*, *Hamamelis* 'Pallida', and a massive block of *Amalanchier candanensis*. On your right, and side by side, are two old yew trees. The fine beech on the left occupies a central point from which paths radiate. (You have an option to turn left if you want a short walk).

Continue down the slight incline, passing a group of *Nothofagus dombeyi* and on the other side is large clump of mature as well as recently planted camellias. Placed haphazardly on both sides of the path are *Acer palmatum* seedlings, some of them named varieties, *Camellia* 'Cornish Snow', *Prunus x subhirtella* 'Autum-

nalis', *Prunus Serrula* with its red peeling bark, *Prunus sargentii*, a tall thin *Gingko biloba*, the green snake-barked *Acer tegmentosa*, and that unmistakable Victorian intruder, the Monkey Puzzle tree. To your left a group of *Magnolia wilsonii* with their beautiful heads dropping downwards have recently been planted, as have *Magnolia* 'Star Wars' and *Magnolia* 'Yellow River'.

At the bench, situated under an ancient magnolia tree, you will see the Weymouth Pine, *Pinus strobus*. Just behind, and thriving in the shade, are *Eucryphia x nymansensis* 'Nymansay' and *Eucryphia x intermedia*. I had been unaware that this acid-loving, very covetable, late-flowering evergreen shrub would grow in our heavy clay ground, so we planted more of them in a sunnier spot opposite.

As you approach this last section and you are walking towards the Cedar of Lebanon, you pass the graceful Western Hemlock and a giant redwood tree that, since it has four straight trunks, may once have been pollarded.

This last section, carpeted with bluebells in the spring, leads to what will become a large yew house. This is my idea: I learnt to smoke in a yew house with a chimney in Scotland, and have always wanted to grow one. This will become, in time, a focal point drawing the eye to the end of the garden. When you reach it, turn round, and you will see what my husband chooses to call a *patte d'oie* – goose foot – paths radiating in five directions. Here you will see how long and thin the garden is. Still with your back to what will become a yew house with a chimney, *Rhododendron luteum*, and *Prunus x yedoensis* straddle all the paths and recently planted *Rhododendron* 'daviesii' with *Tetradium dannielii*, which colours so magnificently, just behind.

Keeping the deer fence on your right, choose another path for your return. The eastern path is lined with Hydrangeas. Named *H. paniculata grandifloras* are planted 'en masse' down to the bench under an oak tree. *Rhododendron* 'Polar Bear' and various species are a little further on. Passing a gate into the Deer Park, you will see a grass circle in which grow *Cornus nuttallii*, the new *Cornus* 'Venus', *Cornus kousa*, *Prunus dulcis*, and *Acer griseum*, punctuated at the end by a yew tree. *Davidia involucrata* is just off the path and various new Rhododendrons, including Mrs Charles Pierson, are gradually being added to the collection. Starting here, on the deer fence side are the peat beds I have already mentioned, which run down to the end of the shrubbery. These still contain some old shrubs, though many of them are overshadowed by yews and other mature trees.

To the left of the path are recently planted *Prunus cerasifera* 'Pissardii' and *Lonicera x purpusii* 'Winter Beauty'. We have planted more magnolias to meet the magnolias seen from the parallel path below. We might one day be able to walk under them down to that lower path.

You should now find yourself at the other side of the large beech tree. Next to it, too close, is *Parottia persica* which turns to such a brilliant orange and red in the autumn. The *Stewartia pseudocamellia* on the old peat side, though not of West Country proportions, is quite respectable, and various *Styrax* were planted to flower in the late summer. *Catalpa bignonioides*, various Magnolias and a fine young Ilex behind the *Syringa x persica* take you towards the house. As you approach you can get a good view of the South Front from the viewing bay. You can see the box parterre planted by my mother-in-law in 1989. This parterre replaced previously unsuccessful attempts and reflects the proportions and harmony of the beautiful façade, possibly inspired by the designs of Inigo Jones who was a contemporary of Robert Cecil and with whom at various times, he had been in touch.

What we have planted is still very immature but our children and grandchildren will enjoy the yew house, as well as the limes, magnolias, and oaks. The joy of Hatfield is that each generation feels able to make its own contribution, marking their stewardship while appreciating what went before.

Nineteenth century 'yew house' in the garden at Keir, Dunblane, Scotland.

The Victorian Kitchen

ELAINE GUNN AND VICKI PERRY

Elaine Gunn (left) and Vicki Perry managed the project to restore the Victorian kitchen in 2009–10. Elaine is the Exhibition and Events Co-ordinator at Hatfield House and recently gained a Masters Degree in the 'The Country House: Art, History and Literature' from Leicester University.

In 2008, Lord Salisbury decided that we would reopen the historic kitchen at Hatfield House. The kitchen was used from the building of the house in 1611 until the beginning of the Second World War and although it was open as a visitors' attraction until the early 1990s it had subsequently become little more than a general storage area.

It was agreed early on that the kitchen would be set in 1846, at the time of Queen Victoria's first visit to Hatfield. After visiting many historic kitchens at other stately homes, we all agreed that it was important to try to achieve a realistic interpretation, with the sights, smells and atmosphere conveying what the kitchen would have been like in Victorian times.

In the nineteenth century many important guests were entertained at Hatfield House; amongst them were writers, politicians, foreign diplomats, heads of state and royalty. Most notable amongst their number was Queen Victoria. The then 2nd Marquess received a letter in early October 1846 announcing that the Queen would be visiting later that month. The royal visit was an immense privilege for the family, while at the same time it was an ordeal to ensure that the Queen enjoyed herself and that all social conventions were upheld, particularly because Lord Salisbury was visiting his Scottish

island of Rum at the time of receiving the letter, and only had ten days to prepare for it. Queen Victoria and Prince Albert stayed with Lord Salisbury and his family for three days, during which time they were extravagantly entertained. The programme consisted of a shooting party and two lavish dinners, the second of which

Two watercolours recording the visit of Queen Victoria to Hatfield in 1846. The one on the left shows the dinner in the Marble Hall, the other the Queen at the ball given for her in the Long Gallery.

The newly restored still room, 2010.

Part of the west wing of the house had burnt down 11 years earlier (killing the Dowager Marchioness of Salisbury) and we have a plan in the archives showing the layout and use of the rooms during the re-building of this wing. We decided that we would need a still room, a scullery and a pastry room as supplemental rooms to the kitchen, as well as restoring the kitchen itself.

Our first task was the physical restoration of the rooms. The work was immense, requiring the installation of a new spiral staircase and the strengthening of the internal walls. The fixtures and fittings of the rooms then had to be put in place. From the plans and our knowledge of historical kitchens, it was clear that the main item missing was a range. In the kitchen itself, ovens had survived from the eighteenth century, along with a fireplace and broken spit. Unfortunately, the original kitchen range had been removed and there was nowhere for the chef to cook his stock and soups! Luckily, an architectural salvage company in Staffordshire had acquired a large Victorian range from a castle in Cheshire, which we bought. It was restored by a local forge and now sits in the kitchen. It will eventually become a working exhibit.

The rooms that were to become the still room and the pastry room were completely bare and a huge amount of imagination and work was required to convert them into part of the exhibit. The pastry room is a cool, north facing room, used by the housekeeper for making pastry, biscuits and cakes. A cold marble slab for making pastry on was donated by a friend of Julie Loughlin's, our Marketing and Media Manager, and custom-built cupboards and work surfaces were built to house the equipment. The still room was where jams, pickles and preserves were made. The still room maid worked in here, under the instruction of the housekeeper and her duties also included baking cakes and making tea and coffee. Tables, work surfaces and a glass-fronted cabinet were made by a carpenter and a fire surround was put into place, along with hooks for the ice picks and aprons.

Certainly one of the most enjoyable parts of restoring the kitchen was acquiring the many items of equipment

was followed by a grand ball, to which 300 guests were invited. The estate workers were not left out of the celebrations; a 96 stone ox was roasted and included in the festivities for them as part of a rustic banquet.

The decision to set the kitchen restoration at the time of Queen Victoria's visit was due to the survival of a lot of archival and other historical material from that period, including newspaper accounts, paintings and household expenses. There are three small ancillary rooms to the kitchen and the archives were particularly important in deciding what these were to be used for.

Copper kettles in the kitchen.

that would have been required for the various staff to use. Inventories in the archives, dating from the mid-nineteenth century, were used to create a shopping list of equipment we needed. Remarkably, we managed to track down the originals of some of the items on our list, for example a 17 inch marble pestle (almost certainly the one that Emma Shotter, the kitchenmaid, would have used in 1846) and an eight day dial clock. Other equipment listed in the inventories had not survived, so part of our task was to trawl local antique shops and eBay to acquire (among other items) a flour tin, a ladle, a copper egg bowl, a preserving pan and a string box. Other items were generously donated by members of staff, including a small Victorian range, belonging to Anthony Downs, our Building Manager, which fitted perfectly into the still room.

Much of the original Victorian copper has fortunately survived, although having been in storage for two decades it required a lot of cleaning. A whole army of volunteers came in during the closed season to help and the copper now looks as shiny as when it was new. The intricately patterned jelly moulds and copper pans are now on display. It took around 140 man-hours to complete the task and we all felt very sorry for the scullery maids who would have been responsible for it in Victorian times.

As well as equipment, real food was important to make the kitchen as realistic as possible. Sugar was sold in a solid form in Victorian times, usually in a conical shape, from which bits were broken off for use in the kitchen. Having found it impossible to acquire a sugar cone in the twenty-first century, we decided to make one ourselves using an old traffic cone, two bags of sugar, a little water and a lot of hard work and pummelling! We also put real vegetables into the scullery; flour and raisins into the pastry room and preserved fruits and jam, made from supermarket jars with their labels soaked off and a fabric cover put on the top, into the still room. Handmade tea towels, with Hatfield House initials embroidered onto them, as would have been the case in former times, completed the equipment and provisions in the newly restored rooms.

So we had our fixtures, fittings and equipment in place; we even had real vegetables. But we also needed to interpret our findings and convey information to those that visited us. We decided we needed to find out more about the people who worked in the kitchens and what they did in them in order to bring the rooms to life. Commissioning touch screens allowed us to do all of this without labelling anything in the kitchen, or putting up boards that would detract from the look and feel of the room as a real working kitchen. An intensive research project ensued, in which our own historical records played a valuable role.

The survival of documents relating to domestic staff can be haphazard at the best of times. At Hatfield we are lucky to have a series of domestic accounts running from 1832 to 1854, which give details of all payments relating to the running of the household. So as well as payments for food and provisions, it also records monthly and quarterly payments made to those people who worked here. In 1846 around 20 full time indoor servants were employed by the 2nd Marquess of Salisbury at Hatfield.

The domestic accounts tell us a little about each staff member, including details of their role, their wages and

Hatfield House domestic staff on the north front steps, ca 1885.

how long they worked for the family. For example, Sidney Hammond, a Hatfield lad, started working as a steward's room boy only six months before the royal visit in 1846. At 16 years old he was the youngest member of staff and was paid £8 per year, the equivalent of a salary of just under a £6,000 today. An inventory from 1848 reveals that his bedroom was in the basement of the house and contained a feather bed, three blankets, a coloured counterpane, a chair and a looking glass.

Some senior servants, such as the chef, lived out of the house, in Estate properties in the town of Hatfield. One of them was Casimir Tessier, Lord Salisbury's French chef, who worked at Hatfield from 1844 until 1851. It was the height of fashion among early Victorian aristocrats to have a French chef, after employment opportunities in France grew thin following the political upheavals of the eighteenth and early nineteenth centuries. Well-known continental chefs such as Alexis Soyer and Charles Francatelli were the celebrity chefs of their day. To employ one was a great indicator of social standing, as they prepared elaborate dishes, artistically designed and well-presented, the cost of which showed that an employer could afford the expense of their upkeep, as well as the quantity and quality of ingredients unattainable to most. Casimir (or Charles as he was known at Hatfield) is recorded in the account books and received an annual salary of £80. This was around five times more than a female British cook in the same position.

Casimir's role was to run the kitchen, undertaking various tasks, such as making stocks, stews and main meals. As a foreign chef, he would have been expected to produce fashionable delicacies, with diverse seasonings and flavours. It is likely that cooking for Queen Victoria was one of the highlights of his career. He almost certainly made turtle soup for the royal visit, as the purchase of turtle is recorded in the domestic account book the previous week. We know from contemporary newspaper accounts that white soup was served for the ball supper, accompanied by iced champagne and brandy. Queen Victoria noted in her diary that she was served coffee after the meal, which was an unusual occurrence at this time. We still have Victorian coffee pots in our kitchens, made out of both silver and copper, one of which may have been used to serve the Queen.

It is difficult to determine what else was consumed by Lord Salisbury and his royal guests during the weekend of the visit, as the menu for the banquet has not survived. However, household accounts listing provisions purchased during the days running up to the visit demonstrate that no expense was spared. The menu would have consisted of copious amounts of extravagant and sumptuous food and drink. It was an expensive affair, with over £11 being spent on champagne (more than the scullery maid's annual salary) and 754 pounds of beef, 1600 eggs and 709 bottles of wine being provided. Distance was also no hindrance to obtaining ingredients; grouse came from Scotland, while from further afield, ice was shipped from Massachusetts to fill the ice house and to assist the chef and confectioner in making jellies and ices.

Casimir was not the only member of staff who would have had his work cut out for him over that particular weekend. Mrs Mary Smith was the housekeeper at Hatfield House between 1833 and 1848 and would have been responsible for making sure the Queen's rooms

The Victorian kitchen, with the original eighteenth century fireplace and ovens on the left.

were maintained to a high standard, as well as being in charge of making tea, cakes and pastry and supervising some of the lower members of staff. As the highest paid female servant, on a salary of just over £25 per year, she was still paid considerably less than her male colleagues. Whether married or not, the female housekeeper was usually known as 'Mrs', a custom that persisted until recent times, with Mrs Hitchcock, the film director Alfred Hitchcock's sister, occupying the position of housekeeper at Hatfield in the 1930s.

One of the most interesting series of documents in the archives regarding the Victorian servants is a series of letters between John Mott, who was the house porter in 1846 and the 2nd Marquess of Salisbury. Although John had worked for the Marquess for over 20 years, he was instantly dismissed following accusations of stealing beer from the cellars at Hatfield House. The letters show his increasing desperation following his dismissal, after which he struggled to find another job without a

Filming for the touch screens – Ceri Ashcroft playing the part of Harriet Smith, scullery maid.

reference. A letter from 1848 says that 'I have nothing but poverty and distress before my eyes, I have now my wife on a bed of sickness and son out of employ and nothing to help myself with.' To which Lord Salisbury replied, 'I am exceedingly sorry that it is impossible for me to acquit you of any guilt in the pilfering of which I complained.' John never worked again, although he was granted an annuity from the Royal Masonic Benevolent Fund Asylum home at Croydon, which must have kept him and his wife from extreme poverty, until his death in 1863.

In order to bring the stories of these servants to life, we decided to get actors to play them, showing the work they did and to put the resulting film on our touch screens. Filming took place in early January 2010. It took two days and the involvement of over 20 people, including eight actors, a costume adviser, a cameraman, a sound engineer and two voice-over artists, not to mention several months of research into the lives and roles of the servant . . . all to create just eight minutes of footage!

The first day of filming began in the vegetable garden, with Colin Hubbard playing John Faircloth, one of the Victorian gardeners. Our own head gardener helped out with the scene and was greatly amused to see us putting carrots into the earth so that Colin could dig them up on camera after having fake mud rubbed into his fingernails! All the other scenes involving the indoor servants were shot inside the house, either in the kitchen and ancillary rooms themselves, or other rooms made to look like a servants' bedroom, housekeeper's office or wine cellar.

One of the most interesting scenes to film was that of John Mott, the porter who was sacked for stealing beer. Joe Cronin gave a compelling performance of his departure and convinced some of us that the real John Mott was innocent of the accusations against him! During filming, we managed to fill the Long Gallery with smoke whilst planning for the kitchen scenes. It was important to show the chef and kitchen maids actually preparing food, which meant lighting the kitchen fire – to which no-one had put a match for several decades. We soon discovered that the kitchen chimney was in dire need of being lined to stop smoke seeping into the Long Gallery upstairs. We were only allowed five minutes of real fire, after which a camping stove was brought in as a replacement to film the bubbling pots! Our great admiration went to Ceri Ashcroft, who really suffered for her art, having had to pluck a real pheasant, supplied by our gamekeeper, despite the fact that she is a vegetarian.

Many of the junior servants had to live in house; the female servants sharing small bedrooms along the top floor corridor, which is portrayed in the clips, and the male servants in the basement. This practice continued right up until the 1930s, according to Flo Wadlow, a former Hatfield kitchen maid. First-hand accounts of these domestic positions are rare, but we are lucky to have a recorded interview with Mrs Wadlow, giving an account of her life in domestic service in Hatfield in the 1930s.

Flo Wadlow (née Copeland) was born in Norfolk in 1913 and in the 1930s she began work as a kitchen maid at Hatfield. Although she was only here for 14 months, her time at Hatfield made a great impression on her and it was a stepping stone to a job at Blicking Hall in Norfolk as Lord Lothian's cook. In August 2009 Mrs Wadlow came back to see the kitchen, which at the time was being restored and also looked around many of the state rooms that she wasn't allowed to enter as a young kitchen maid. Flo had many stories about her time at Hatfield and kindly allowed us to record her as she reminisced. When she started work, there was already someone who used the name Flo, so she was told she had to use her middle name to avoid confusion. However her middle name, Georgina, was considered to be too posh and she was known as 'Ena' by the rest of the staff! She enjoyed going to chapel most mornings (except when she was on breakfast duty) and recalled that this was the only place that she had the opportunity to see the then Marquess and Marchioness (the current Lord Salisbury's great grandparents). She also used to volunteer to clean the floor of the Armoury, just so that she could see the Four Seasons tapestries, which were on display there at the time.

Flo's interview was put onto two 1930s telephones, which visitors can use in the kitchen to listen to her stories. Although Flo clearly was not a Victorian kitchen maid, she is a real life link with the kitchen's past and was able to make us understand what it was like to work here in a way that we never could from reading books or studying in the archives.

Our vision for the kitchen was to make it as authentic an experience as possible for visitors, so that they can really feel as though they are in a Victorian service wing.

Lord Salisbury and Florence Wadlow (née Copeland, former kitchen maid), August 2009.

As far as possible, the kitchen is laid out as it would have been in the nineteenth century, with real food, a working fire and spit and even a smell machine that wafts a realistic Victorian odour into the room. The project has been a great success and the introduction of a servants' area adds a new dimension to the house. We hope that visitors enjoy seeing what life was like for a Victorian servant.

HATFIELD HOUSE

Kevin Dean, the Hatfield House Chef, has prepared two menus for four people, which are healthy, inexpensive, quick and easy to prepare. The ingredients come mostly from the Estate; game and pigeon from the woods, blackberries from the hedgerows, local trout, eggs, peaches and vegetables from the garden. Almost always, Kevin uses what he calls 'our own'.

*Kevin Dean with his assistant,
Miss Martha Campbell.*

MENU I

*Warm Game and Smoked Duck Salad
with Balsamic Dressing*

Pigeon with Orange and Sherry Sauce

Blackberry Fool

MENU 2

Grilled Vegetables on Ciabatta Toast

Pan-fried Trout with Hollandaise Sauce

Hot Whole Peaches in Syrup with cream

Warm Game and Smoked Duck Salad with Balsamic Dressing

INGREDIENTS

Mixed Game birds: partridge, pheasant, smoked duck (from Farmers' Market) Bacon Lardons Cooked globe artichokes in brine or oil Mixed salad leaves or rocket	Dressing: 1 cup Balsamic oil 1 garlic clove 2 cups Olive oil ¼ tsp each dry tarragon, parsley and thyme Mix in a glass jar and give a good shake. Not all will be used and it will keep.

METHOD

When cooking Game, keep it simple. This dish can be eaten warm or cold but serving warm brings out the gamey flavour. I use only the breasts, taken off the carcass.

Just season with salt and pepper and cook in a hot pan for about 3 minutes each side; leave to cool in the pan.
In another pan, fry the lardons, add drained artichokes (one per person) and leave to stand in the pan.

Dress the plate with salad leaves, add cooked and sliced game and smoked duck, sprinkle lardons and artichokes on top and drizzle dressing over. Serve at once.

Roast Pigeon Crowns with Orange and Dry Sherry Sauce Wrapped in Bacon

INGREDIENTS

4 Crowns of Pigeon 4 rashers streaky bacon 1 orange cut into quarters ¼ pint Dry Sherry ¼ pint of stock Butter, olive oil Salt and pepper	Mixed to a paste with a little oil: 2 large shallots, chopped 4 juniper berries, crushed ¼ tbsp. dried mixed herbs 2 cloves garlic, crushed

METHOD

Rub herb and garlic mixture into pigeon crowns.

Place the quarter of orange in the crown and wrap the bacon around the breast; secure with a cocktail stick.

Heat a pan which can go in the oven, add oil and butter and fry to colour all sides of the crown. Remove from pan.

Add shallots and cook till soft, add sherry, bring to the boil and add the stock.

Place crowns in the pan and bring back to the boil. Put pan

into a hot oven 160°C for about an hour. (less time for pink meat, more for dry).

Take cooked birds out and check seasoning of sauce. Sauce can be poured over or served separately.

Blackberry Fool

INGREDIENTS

1lb fresh blackberries
2½ oz caster sugar
8fl oz cream

Pastry cream:
12 fl oz milk
1 cap vanilla essence
4 egg yokes
1 oz plain flour
Knob of butter

METHOD

Make pastry cream first: bring milk to boiling point add vanilla essence, leave to cool for 10 minutes.

Whisk egg yolks and sugar until light and fluffy, add flour and give a good whisk.

Pour milk onto egg mixture and mix gently. Return to pan, then heat bringing it back to the boil, then simmer; stirring for 2-3 minutes or until it coats the back of the spoon. Take off the heat and leave to cool.

*NB You may not need all the pastry cream; it will depend on how sweet you like your puddings.

In a heavy pan, add the blackberries, sugar and a splash of water and bring to the boil. Simmer until the fruit is soft.

You can blitz and pass through a sieve if you prefer a smooth texture or leave it with bits. Leave to cool.

Whip cream to soft peak. Fold blackberry sauce into pastry cream (to taste), then fold in the cream. Serve in individual dishes or one bowl.

Chill and Serve with almond thins (biscuits) with berries to garnish.

Grilled Vegetables on Ciabatta Toast with goats cheese, served with rocket pesto

INGREDIENTS

Depending upon the season or to taste: Tomato, red pepper, garlic, mushrooms, courgette, globe artichoke, aubergine.
4 good slices of Ciabatta
4 good slices of goats cheese
Olive Oil to drizzle.

Sauce:
125gm bag of rocket
Handful of pine nuts
Handful of grated parmesan
1 clove garlic crushed
¼ pint olive oil
Seasoning to taste.

METHOD

Toast bread on both sides, set aside. Slice cheese and place one on each piece of toast.

Cook vegetables of your choice either on a griddle pan or under the grill. Place on top of ciabatta and goats cheese. Drizzle with olive oil and bake in the oven for around 5 minutes.

Sauce: Mix all ingredients with a magi-mix stick or pulser. Pour over hot toast and serve.

Pan-fried Trout with Hollandaise Sauce

INGREDIENTS

4 Trout fillets
1tsp capers
¼tsp fish spice

Pinch of dry English mustard
Black pepper (a few twists)
Knob of butter

METHOD

Pat dry fillets, season with all the above. Heat a pan and add the knob of butter. Place flesh side down and cook for 1 minute. Turn over and cook for a few more minutes; skin should be crisp. Take off the heat and serve with hollandaise sauce.

Game and Smoked Duck Salad.

Hot Whole Peaches in Syrup with cream

INGREDIENTS

4 whole white peaches
2 Star Anise
1 stick of cinnamon
4 cloves

¼ pint of water
4oz sugar
2oz apricot jam

METHOD

Bring water and sugar to the boil, add cinnamon, star anise and cloves. Boil for 10 minutes.

Add the peaches (you my skin them if you wish) and apricot jam; again, bring to the boil.

Simmer for 10-15 minutes until soft. Remove from pan. Reduce sauce until it covers the back of the spoon or single cream consistency.

Pour over peaches and serve with cream or ice-cream.

Lady Gwendolen Cecil

HANNAH SALISBURY

Hannah Salisbury edited David Cecil, A Portrait by his Friends, *a collection of essays about her husband's great uncle. The historian and biographer Sir Kenneth Rose has generously allowed her to quarry and plunder from his book* The Later Cecils. *Lord David Cecil's book,* The Cecils of Hatfield House, *is quoted at length.*

ALTHOUGH Lady Gwendolen Cecil was born 40 years before Queen Victoria died, I was lucky enough to have enjoyed endless stories of her charm originality and intelligence from her nephew Lord David Cecil. Both Lady Gwendolen and the young David lived at Hatfield, she because she never left, and he because he was a delicate and nervous child who therefore spent his entire childhood with his mother, and in the company of his entertaining aunts and uncles. They listened to his precocious opinions, but these opinions had to be defended: when he was seven years old, David was asked by his uncle Linky what he thought the purpose of life was. His answer was that he thought it was to make people happy. Lord Hugh's enraged response was 'any competent licensed victualler could do as much.'

The 3rd Marquess of Salisbury had himself suffered a sad and lonely childhood after his mother had died when he was nine years old. However, he and his wife Georgina and their seven children made Hatfield into an unusually happy family home. The two eldest children were girls: Lady Maud who was born in 1858 and Lady Gwendolen in 1860. There followed five sons: 'Jem', later 4th Marquess of Salisbury, born in 1861, Lord William, known as Fish, in 1863, then Lord Robert, called Bob, born in 1864, followed by Lord Edward, known as Nigs, in 1867. Finally Lord Hugh, known as Linky was born in 1869. Unconsciously eccentric, tales of family life were legion. They never stopped talking. They argued endlessly on the most abstruse subjects,

Two sisters, Maud and Gwendolen Cecil, photographed by Lewis Carroll in his sitting-room at Christ Church, Oxford, 1870.

and with their father virtually running his administration from Hatfield, (he was Foreign Secretary and then Prime Minister for much of the period 1878–1902) these clever, confident, unworldly siblings witnessed the hard grind of practical politics at the coal face.

Staying at Hatfield was all very well for those who could take it. Kenneth Rose wrote, 'Those who lacked the stamina of the Cecils found their perpetual debates, often on the most trivial of topics, both a bore and a strain' and this was confirmed by Eleanor Cecil, Lord Robert's wife: 'Chiffon women are dull and tiresome but they don't try to knock one down over a difference in the weather! I sometimes feel as if I must scream if some argument is gone on with for one more minute.' Meals were endless, always late, and with 'far too much food of rich and not too safe quality.'

Health was a subject for intense concern, and their hypochondria was nurtured by continuous recourse to the medicine chest and taking their temperatures for no reason other than that they thought they were going to be ill. Amongst these martyrs to the thermometer, two lived to be nonagenarians and four lived well into their eighties, but it was unsurprising that they didn't feel especially well at Hatfield.

Punctuality was never a virtue practised by either Gwendolen's mother or her children. Salisbury used to say that 'while waiting for his wife to come down to dinner he had read right through the Church Fathers.' Gwendolen suited this cerebral, masculine world; they were all intensely religious and disquisitions from Linky, argued over with Gwendolen, were presumably the cause of some of those endless meals.

Lord Salisbury did not believe in higher education for women. This was to have tragic consequences for Gwendolen as she was highly intelligent and a university education would have given her a breadth and intellectual discipline which would have sustained and helped her to complete her father's political biography. Lord David in his book *The Cecils of Hatfield House* wrote 'She was an extraordinary mixture of simplicity and wisdom. For, along with an incurable innocence that led her to believe improbable tales of misfortune, she

Prime Minister Salisbury, photographed in about 1900.

Pencil and watercolour drawing of Lady Gwendolen Cecil by M. E. Hall.

without indifference: the Duke of Norfolk, a widower 13 years her senior and brother of her closest friend, Lady Margaret Howard. Salisbury thought highly enough of the Duke to make him Postmaster-General in the administration of 1895–1900, but would hardly have welcomed his daughter's betrothal to the lay leader of England's Roman Catholics. The proposed match, if such it was, remained no more than a whispered family legend.'

In 1899 when Lady Salisbury died, Gwendolen effectively committed her life to that of her father. The years of unselfish devotion she gave her parents ended in 1903 with his death. It was a devastating loss. He had meant everything to her. But she was to enter a new stage in her life. Her brother Jem, now 4th Marquess, gave her the delightful Lodge House in the Park and 'with her deliverance from domestic thraldom came both rejuvenation and a fulfilment of intellectual promise. She was consulted, revered, and loved' and any residual pretence to convention finally went by the board now that she had her own home. Sixty years later, talking to Kenneth Rose, some Cecil and Palmer nephews and nieces delightedly recalled her innocent eccentricities: the fervour with which she played the piano or read aloud, unruly pince-nez tinkling against a battery of brooches; the

possessed an unusually powerful intellect – my grandfather thought her the cleverest of his children – always working at full pitch, reflecting, analysing, drawing interesting conclusions on religion, on social reform, on politics. Her political judgement was penetrating . . .'

After her elder sister Maud married, Gwendolen was required to share with her mother in the running of the household and Estate. She identified her life wholly with her father's, for whom she acted as a sort of unofficial and confidential private secretary and became to her parents their constant and indispensable companion.

Gwendolen never married. In Sir Kenneth Rose's perceptive and sparkling biography *The Later Cecils* he wrote, 'On only one suitor was she suspected of smiling

The Lodge House, rebuilt in 1651 for Philip Cecil, Keeper of Hatfield Little Park. It was Lady Gwendolen's home from 1907 until her death in 1945.

Lady Gwendolen Cecil in a battery-driven electric car outside Hatfield House in 1903. With her are her nieces, Beatrice and Mary Cecil, and her nephew, George Cecil, who was later to be killed in action in the first month of the Great War.

familiar posture of kneeling before the fire, close enough on one alarming occasion for the combs on her hair to start smouldering; her disregard for schoolroom routine or the approaching shadow of bedtime; the eloquent intensity she brought to themes as various as the causes of European unrest or the best way to wash a dog.

Gwendolen never cared much for clothes, nor was she prepared to make concessions with her appearance; she was short-sighted, painfully shy, and lacked self confidence when not at Hatfield or with her family. She dreaded social occasions. In Cairo, staying with her brother she wrote 'the nervous strain of continuous small talk here is terrific. It's appalling to think that if I had married my life might have been always in such conditions. What dreadful fates a merciful Heaven saves one from.' Her sister-in-law Nelly Cecil recalled her striking appearance as Portia 'She looked splendid. It gave one an idea of what a little more attention might have done: she had beautiful hair, a warm brown with gold lights in it and an attractive wave.' She was not to

give 'a little more attention' to her appearance. Viewing with alarm a proposed visit by the King and Queen, Gwendolen wrote 'I am going to shirk as much as I can and am feeling very republican . . . if I avoid them Saturday, one new skirt to match a blouse I've got will meet the occasion.'

Her niece, Lady Manners, wrote:

She either thought a lot about her clothes, or not at all. When she thought – and we were kept up in the progress of the scheme – it was not only to invent an Admiral Crichton sort of garment, whose top could be worn by day or in the evening, but it would be made by a distressed dressmaker. The skirt would be a remnant her secretary had bought for her. This would gratify the secretary and the conjunction of aiding, pleasing and being useful was delightful. If only the blouse could be used as a sponge as well, it certainly would have been adopted. But on the whole she did not think about clothes, so she would wear black stockings with brown shoes and brown stockings with black shoes. The stockings wrinkled and the shoes untied. Two or three really good diamond brooches would be pinned on anyhow. If she had a good tweed, the hat would be her wedding hat. Her hats were of the same type. Anyway after a short time they were battered into the same type, though some reached such fame as to be nicknamed by the family – Bersaglieri was one. Bersaglieri blew off into the sea, was retrieved sodden, and clapped on again, her remarking 'not much the worse'.

Lady Gwendolen was a familiar sight in the Park. Parish visiting and neighbourly duties were very much encouraged by her mother, but what concerned her most was the housing of the poor, the old, and the infirm. She became an able architect and her beautifully drawn plans and very precise calculations were used to build some of the Estate houses which can still be seen around Hatfield today.

Apart from this, Gwendolen's creative years had largely been wasted but it was in 1906 that she embarked on her great work – writing the official life of her father. 'Though I could never make such a fine work of it as Linky would do, I frankly believe I understand him better' Gwendolen told her brother Bob. The task she set herself was immense. Sir Eric Barrington, who was her father's Principal Private Secretary, sent down the whole of his private correspondence – that amounted to the fourteen years of his tenure of the Foreign Office. The archives, mostly unsorted, arrived in 'filthy packing cases, with all the elastic bands broken and the piles mixed'. Forty volumes of Hansard only brought Gwendolen's background reading up to 1885 added to which were all the diplomatic despatches, blue books, files of newspapers and articles from the *Quarterly Review.* 'When once I have plunged into the work I feel I shall be lost to human sight for years to come' she said.

David Cecil wrote:

Although she spent forty years at this task, she never finished it, partly because she had a lust for perfection which led her to revise and scrap and rewrite again and again, and partly because she allowed herself frequently to be distracted – it might be by a book she picked up casually which instantly absorbed her whole attention, but more often by some appeal to her compassionate heart, easily inflamed to forget all else in a desire to relieve suffering. A beggar-woman met on a walk who told her a tale of woe, a letter from an unknown lunatic complaining that he was unjustly confined in an asylum: these were enough to make my aunt throw all her work aside in order to get wrong righted. How often do I remember her arriving at Hatfield House at any hour of day or night, on fire with pity and indignation, to pour out vividly and at length some story of this kind into the sympathetic but sceptical ears of my father and mother! She had an especially soft spot for lunatics; and her efforts on their behalf were so strenuous that she sometimes got them released. More often than not, it was soon found necessary to send them back to the asylum. So also did the beggar-woman often turn out an unworthy object of my aunt's charity. This did not stop her from believing the next hard-luck story she heard and taking up the cause of the next discontented madman who might come her way.

Finally, and notwithstanding her many interests and distractions, Gwendolen published the first two volumes of her magnum opus in 1921 and wrote in November: 'I have certainly had a wonderful press . . . I was surprised to see, repeated in one notice after another, how much of what the critics read was a revelation to them. A kind of myth had grown up of the haughty and rather inhuman and cold aristocrat . . . One is pleased naturally at having one's work praised – but it is a far deeper and more enduring cause for thankfulness that one has been the instrument of making him and the lesson of his life known to others.'

Gwendolen was 61-years-old when she published the first two volumes. She was about to embark on the events of the 1880s which were the years when she had been at the very heart of affairs. Her personal recollections undoubtedly increased the fascination of her work, but may have added to the burden of her labours. Each year of her father's administration took her one year to complete.

Undaunted, she soldiered on, publishing two further volumes in 1931 and 1932. These only took her to 1892. On her death she left behind ten draft chapters of an uncompleted fifth and final volume. Gwendolen Cecil's unfinished life of her father is still seen as one of the great political biographies in the language.

Textiles in the House

JOAN KENDALL

Joan Kendall qualified in textile design and technology and is also a costume historian specialising in the cut and construction of historic dress. She was trained in textile conservation techniques by members of the Textile Conservation Department of the Victoria and Albert Museum.

THE TEXTILE CONSERVATION GROUP at Hatfield House was created in 1977 when I was asked to bring together and train skilled volunteers to conserve the historic textiles on display in the areas of the House open to the general public. The House had been neglected when it was a hospital during the Second World War and there was a considerable amount of work to be done to nearly all the textiles which remained. Needlewomen with good, accurate stitching skills were invited to apply and to be taught to use the textile conservation methods of the Victoria and Albert Museum. Ideally they were to attend, with travelling expenses paid, one day a week or one a fortnight.

There was such an overwhelming response of about 250 replies to the letters sent out to various groups, including the Embroiderers' Guild, the Guild of Weavers, Spinners and Dyers, the W.I, and NADFAS that, although the primary necessity was to conserve the unique early seventeenth century Four Seasons tapestries it became possible to have, in addition to the tapestry section, others dealing with embroideries, lace, upholstery and miscellaneous objects such as saddles and bridles, as well as cataloguing, cleaning and storing objects correctly.

Although the group is now much smaller than the 80 to 90 founder members there are still those who have been here since the beginning of the project, or who joined soon afterwards, whose dedication and skills are greatly valued by Lord and Lady Salisbury. It is important to note that without the encouragement and teaching of the correct methods by the Textile Conservation Department of the Victoria and Albert Museum the project would not have been possible.

When there was an exciting opportunity to research the history of and to conserve the Bed of State in the private side of the House, which was in a room where it was not possible to invite the general public, group

Joan Kendall with some members of the Textile Conservation Team. The Tudor Rose table carpet can be seen on the further frame, whilst the Brussels tapestry on the table is being prepared for re-hanging on the Grand Staircase by enclosing the worn edges with new woollen ribbed fabric.

Spring is the first of the Four Seasons tapestries which were woven in England at the time of the building of Hatfield House. The idea of the seated figure representing the Season was adopted from a set of engravings by Martin de Vos, but the countryside and all that is happening within it was designed just for this tapestry – as were the details in the other three Seasons. The borders of emblematic pictures with quotations are not found in any other tapestry.

Solvit in Lacrimas Cor, or 'A Heart Melts into Tears', is one of the emblems in the lower border of Winter. The dark woollen outlines defining the objects and also the lettering had rotted and disappeared but by stitching within the spaces which were left the design and motto became clear.

Celebrating May Day is a detail from Spring. A bagpiper with a crown of flowers is leading a man and woman in colourful clothing who carry bunches of blossoms and wear headdresses of flowers.

In Summer the sheep are being washed in the river before shearing. The pale area in the river is a new patch replacing an earlier one which had been cut from another tapestry and which was visually distracting. As there was no evidence of the original weaving an outline suggestion of the rest of the sheep and ripples of water was stitched on the patch to blur the plain coloured area. Note the lion in the top left corner.

The pair of rabbits, one disappearing into a burrow and one alert before coming out, also from Summer, is one of the many amusing details to look for in all the Four Seasons tapestries.

In this detail of Autumn baskets of gathered grapes are being tipped into a covered area where two men leaning on poles for balance are walking around treading the grapes. The juice runs out at the front into barrels which the cooper is sealing with a bung and a barrel is taken away on a wheeled cart. The carter on his horse is flirting with a girl who, hand on hip, carries a basket on her head.

Winter brings a Storm at Sea with a man falling out of one of the ships into a sea full of monsters. The people on the shore are exclaiming in horror or praying and even the little town tucked in a hollow is being battered as the storm clouds rage over it.

members were pleased to be able to involved in such interesting work.

The elaborately phrased original bill dated 1711 was in the archives. It included the complete furnishing of the room with the costs of every item in detail even including nails and screws and the wages of the men who put it all together. The crimson handwoven silk damask with which the room was furnished was of a triumphal arch in a garden with pretty pavilions, parterres and flower beds and a splendidly elaborate fountain. The repeat of the design measures 1.65 metres and the width is 55 cms. It was almost certainly woven in Spitalfields to a design by James Leman as it includes many details from a book of his designs held in the Victoria and Albert Museum.

This led to working on four other important beds and involvement in many other schemes throughout the rest of the House, including designing and producing a number of embroidery kits and an Elizabethan lace pricking for sale in the shop all based on items in the House.

TAPESTRIES

Of greatest interest because they are unique is the set of the Four Seasons woven in England and attributed to the Sheldon tapestry workshop at Barcheston in Warwickshire. As the shield above each tapestry indicates they were probably commissioned by Sir John Tracy of Toddington in Gloucestershire sometime after his marriage to Anne Shirley in 1590 and finished by 1611 or 1612. We know this because the year 1611 is woven halfway along the upper border of Winter. They were woven in wool, silk, linen, silver gilt metal threads and Dutch gold across woollen warps, and were a brilliant acquisition by the 2nd Marquess in the nineteenth century.

Each tapestry has a dominant, very large main figure symbolising that Season seated in a landscape filled with country people working or celebrating as they would have done in England at the turn of the seventeenth century. This is within a border containing a series of roundels, each showing a scene from the Bible or ancient classical literature or taken from a book of Emblems each enclosed by a vine or rope and surrounded by flowers and fruits.

Although there is a wide difference in the technical skills of the individual weavers involved, this creates the charm and naivety of the scenes. The central figures are by a highly skilled weaver who probably specialised in this difficult discipline. The flowers, fruits and vegetables are recognisably woven but there are many oddities in the perspective and proportions of the people, birds and animals and it is fun to look carefully to identify these.

Western tapestries of this period were woven by hand on a large loom sideways and from behind, the front of the design being on the surface away from the weaver. He would copy a full size drawing or 'cartoon', the outlines of which would be drawn on the warps, the strong vertical threads. The weavers did not pass the finer weft threads across the whole width of the warps on the loom using a shuttle as in weaving cloth, but wove only small detailed areas using a series of bobbins each with its own coloured weft thread. These areas were linked together either by twisting the two adjacent weft threads during weaving or by stitching together the two adjacent warp threads after the areas had been woven.

When complete the tapestry would be cut off the loom and turned by 90 degrees so the design was the correct way up. This meant that it would now hang from the thinner threads, the wefts, putting them under physical strain which, combined with damage caused by exposure to light, resulted in weakened and broken wefts, fading of dye colour and loss of some of the dark woollen outlines which define the objects.

By the end of the nineteenth century the Four Seasons Tapestries had deteriorated considerably and Autumn was eventually sent for repair by the 4th Marquess to the William Morris Company where the damaged areas were re-woven. The work did not take into account the distinctive style and colouring of the original and was considered to have changed the tapestry unacceptably so the other three Seasons were not sent away for repair. Since then sailcloth patches have been inserted behind

This section of the third emblem down in the right hand border of Spring *shows a typically damaged area with holes, distorted and broken warps and missing wefts. The damage has been caused by insect infestation, damp conditions, exposure to light and incorrect dyeing methods. The net which protected this area during wet cleaning has been removed but another section of net protecting the outer edge of the tapestry is still stitched in place.*

holes and worn areas and groups of loose warps were stitched down to the lining by household staff. This held the tapestries together until we were able to conserve them fully using the methods recommended by the Textile Conservation Department of the Victoria and Albert Museum.

All repair stitches holding a tapestry to its lining were carefully cut away and about 250 patches were removed from each one.

After checking for possible dye bleeding, particularly from the wools and silks used in repairs over the years, each tapestry was encased in strong net for overall support and wet cleaned by hand on a flat surface using the correct Victoria and Albert Museum washing formula and cleaning techniques.

The tapestry was then mounted on a three beam frame to be supported by stitching onto a complete sheet of open weave linen. Where there were large holes, a specially dyed piece of ribbed cotton textile was stitched under each hole. In areas where warps were broken or missing for a short length a new specially

This section of the border of the Tudor Rose Table Carpet, taken before conservation, shows, as well as the typical Tudor Rose motif, two mottoes 'Sta(n)ding pools gather fylthe' and 'Rening water ever sweet'. The Rose is 14 cms high and the whole carpet measures 2.56 metres by 2.59 metres.

These motifs on a Long Cushion are worked in tent stitch with silk on fine canvas before being cut out and stitched on to a velvet ground.

TOP *A butterfly perched on honeysuckle is surrounded by a snail, a flying lizard and a caterpillar with a cornflower beside it.*

BELOW *A monkey with a red cap sits on an oak tree. On the left is a caterpillar near a snail and a bee.*

spun woollen warp thread was inserted over the gap and each end stitched securely between the tapestry and the support linen.

All stitching had to be of the correct tension so that when it was hung the tapestry would not be physically distorted. All conservation stitching must not be more noticeable than the original weaving and it must be capable of being removed at a later date without damaging the original.

The very many areas of bare warps where the fine weft threads had broken were stitched down over alternate warps to the support linen in bricked parallel lines 1/8th inch apart. Two colour-blended threads of spun polyester, which has the same elasticity as silk and will last much longer, were used to replace threads which were originally silk, and one thread of crewel wool was used to replace previous woollen wefts. Where there was no indication of original colour, neutral warp coloured threads were used.

As some areas of the design were completely missing, we depended on a set of large plate black and white photographic prints, taken probably around the turn of the twentieth century, for details which had been lost since then. The prints are of such excellent quality that individual warps can be distinguished with a magnifying glass. Using this information to plot out the design, the missing areas of weft were indicated with stitches. Many of the outlines which were missing were surrounded by firmly woven wool allowing the space to be filled in accurately with a new dark outline. This method revealed the missing quotations linked to the roundels in the border. The photographs showed a number of large holes which had already been patched with non-matching pieces cut from other tapestries. These were not replaced during conservation.

If the new plain coloured patches which we dyed to blend were too visually distracting, using the photographs if possible for evidence, an indication of the missing design was stitched on to the patch. The worn tapestry outer borders were mounted on a specially woven woollen rep, and the tapestry was lined and hung using Velcro mesh tape to give even support.

During this process there was found half way down the right hand borders of only Spring and Winter, the first and the last of the set to be woven, the remains of a woven depiction of a tapestry weaver's bobbin filled with golden coloured thread. As a bobbin is used as a weaver's mark for the city of Bruges it could imply that someone, maybe the highly skilled weaver of the figures, was trained in Bruges.

Divided between a number of rooms in the House is a set of 19 tapestries woven in the last quarter of the seventeenth century in Brussels with the mark of one of the most important workshops, that of Hendrik Reydams. They illustrate myths of the Greek and Roman gods, goddesses and heroes. Technically they are very fine and because they were in demand there were many sets woven at that time.

Lord Salisbury has recently completely changed the character of the King James Drawing Room by hanging a series of paintings against walls full of mostly Aubusson tapestries in a decorative style formerly very fashionable. The classic example was in the Long Gallery at Hardwick Hall in Derbyshire. These tapestries are principally Verdures, containing scenes of wild or tame animals and birds in a park landscape, with trees, lakes and streams and sometimes with formal gardens, follies or pavilions in the distance. They are complemented by the superb green silk velvet of the curtains and upholstery stamped with a large Renaissance design and made, as are the other curtains in the House, by hand at Hatfield.

EMBROIDERIES

A number of early embroideries of the late sixteenth or early seventeenth centuries remain in the House, mostly showing signs of having been in use for a considerable period, and therefore of having been much appreciated by successive generations of the Cecil family. Each of these has been or will be stitched onto a suitable support textile to help to prevent further damage.

The most fragile and largest embroidery is the Tudor Rose table carpet, dating from no later than 1603. The centre of the carpet is a formalised design of carnation flower heads and decorative crosses. The borders contain Tudor roses and stylised flower heads alternating with cartouches enclosing mottoes or quotations. When new it was very long and narrow. Later, when it had become very worn one of the long side borders had been cut away, the remaining area which was in reasonable condition was cut across into two equal lengths which were stitched together side by side and part of the spare side border was added to each end. It is now being supported on linen.

As well as other smaller table carpets there are long cushions which were mainly for display and were often placed across the arms of chairs for decoration. Some are composed of 'slips', which are details of plants, animals or insects, worked on very fine canvas in silk or wool, then cut out and appliquéd to a velvet ground.

Among other items of this date are some delightful panels of goldwork showing peapods and mirror images of Ss embroidered on fine red silk velvet probably from bed hangings.

The Merman valance, also probably from a set of bed hangings, shows a repeating pattern of 'grotesques'. It is most interesting because the embroidery has worn so much in places that it has been possible to extract two of the papers which had been used to support the raised work. It appears to be from an account book but is not easily identifiable.

The early seventeenth century laces in the family collection include the figure of a merman and dolphins possibly taken from the same series of books of designs

Grotesque Mermen with entwined tails face each other alternately along the remains of the 38 cm deep upper valance from what must have been a dramatic set of bed hangings from the end of the sixteenth century. They are stitched with silk and 'gold' thread in long and short stitch, basketwork and raised work padded with twists of very fine paper, two of which can be seen exposed at the bottom right hand side.

The King Merman needle lace panel is 14 cm high. It is made by working in a variety of buttonhole stitches above a paper design. The breathing gills show clearly on either side of the king's chest and the dolphin like sea creatures beside each trident spout streams of water from their mouths.

as the embroidered Merman valance. These books were used as design sources for needlework of all kinds as well as for carvings, painted and other decorative surfaces such as can be seen in the Marble Hall and on the case of the organ in the Armoury.

UPHOLSTERY

A number of seventeenth century padded chairs around the House as well as very many later sofas, chairs and stools have been re-upholstered and re-covered many times using only traditional techniques.

Amongst them is Queen Anne's Chair of State, a carved and gilded chair with footstool originally upholstered in cloth of gold and silver with a Bizarre design in primary colours. It must have gleamed wonderfully during the Coronation Ceremony in Westminster Abbey in 1702. Traces of this textile were found underneath fragments of ten other later re-coverings when the chair was re-upholstered by the Furniture Department of the Victoria and Albert Museum in 1959.

At the request of the 5th Marquess a length of antique Genoese cut and uncut voided silk velvet in crimson and white was used and the chair was trimmed with elaborate crimson tasselled and buttoned gold-trimmed braid originally used in the State bedroom. As this fragile velvet quickly suffered considerable deterioration partly due to the flexing of the textile on a soft surface, the covering was removed and stitched down to a firm linen support and then re-applied to the chair where the support textile is now barely noticeable through the holes.

The eight backstools from the State bedroom and four other backstools of similar date are being re-gilded before being covered in new silk damask to be woven to the original 1711 garden design used in the State bedroom. The original horsehair and linen upholstery is in good condition and can continue to be used.

FUTURE EXHIBITION OF HISTORIC TEXTILES

At the moment it is not possible for the fragile early textiles to be accessible to visitors. However, there are future plans to provide a room to display some of the House's remarkable collection of textiles.

The Queen Anne Chair of State after conservation of the antique Genoese 'cut and uncut' silk velvet. It may once have had a matching feather cushion for the seat, but even without one is most comfortable.

The Archives – digitisation project

VICKI PERRY

Vicki Perry has worked in the Archives at Hatfield House for almost five years. She qualified as an archivist at University College, Dublin in 2003, after winning the Archival Studentship at the National Library of Ireland in 2001–2.

B Y THE TIME Hatfield House was completed in 1611, Robert Cecil, the 1st Earl of Salisbury, had already had a long and successful political career, in which he followed his father, William Cecil, Lord Burghley. These two men dominated Elizabethan politics, holding various public appointments including Secretary of State and Lord High Treasurer. The official roles, which they performed during the reigns of Elizabeth I and James I (and VI of Scotland), are documented in a collection of manuscripts held in the archives at Hatfield House, known as the Cecil Papers.

The Cecil Papers are those documents that Lord Burghley and Robert Cecil wrote, received and accumulated during the course of their political careers and that were in the possession of Robert Cecil on his death (including papers left to him by his father). Following Burghley's death in 1598, the papers were kept at Salisbury House, Robert Cecil's London property, along with documents relating to the family's estates and properties. When Salisbury House was pulled down after the death of the 4th Earl in 1694, the papers were moved to Hatfield, where they have remained for over 300 years.

The sixteenth and early seventeenth centuries were a time of great political and constitutional change. Events such as the marriages of Henry VIII, the execution of

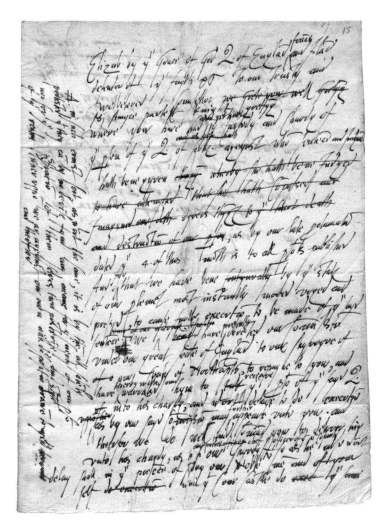

Lord Burghley's rough draft of the warrant ordering the execution of Mary Queen of Scots, 1586 (Cecil Papers 165/10).

Mary Queen of Scots, the re-conquest of Ireland, the Gunpowder Plot and the Spanish Armada irrevocably changed the course of British history and in some cases the effects of these events can still be felt today. The Cecil Papers contain manuscripts relating to all of this dynamic period, and are invaluable for understanding the events of this era.

The collection contains a number of highlights, including a draft warrant for the execution of Mary Queen of Scots, a proclamation on the accession of James I and letters from Walter Raleigh, Francis Walsingham, Francis Drake and Robert Dudley. Amongst these historically important documents are hidden gems, which whilst not as notable, give a glimpse into the lives and beliefs of those writing them. A letter written in 1587 by Richard Carmerden to Elizabeth I regarding a cup to be presented to the Queen states that *we take the cup to be of unicorn's horn, which, if it so be, is a most rare jewel for the greatness of it*. Alexander Bonus, writing in 1589, offers to *convert mercury into pure gold; to make 5 oz. of perfect gold at the cost of an angel; to convert silver into perfect gold at small expense, and all in a very short space of time*, in exchange for Sir Francis Walsingham, the recipient, agreeing to release him from prison. Also included in the collection are a number of long pedigrees of Lord Burghley who, maybe feeling rather put out by some contemporaries saying that his grandfather 'kept the best inn in Stamford' commissioned them to show a (probably fictitious) descent from an ancient Welsh family by the name of Sitsylt.

One of the most important jobs of an archivist is cataloguing and arranging collections of manuscripts, so that individual documents can be easily located by researchers. The Cecil Papers were catalogued by Charles James Stewart, a London bookseller between 1829 and 1831, a task that took him 371 days according to contemporary records. The manuscripts were unfolded and pressed, and placed into calf-bound volumes. Several years later, additional papers were discovered and were bound into further volumes and a catalogue of the entire collection was produced and published by the Historical

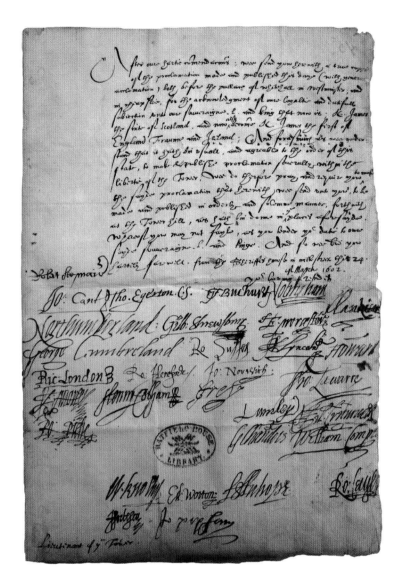

Proclamation of the Accession of King James, 1603
(Cecil Papers 99/43).

Manuscripts Commission in 24 volumes.

As well as describing the contents of each individual document in a collection, an archivist should arrange a collection in order to put the documents into context in relation to other documents. Often, the circumstances in which documents were written and their relationship to each other tells us as much as the content of the

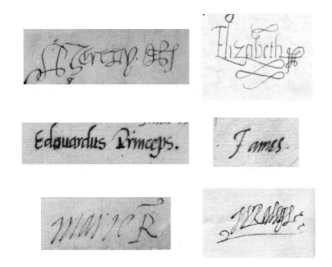

Famous signatures from the Cecil Papers: King Henry VIII, King Edward VI, Queen Mary, Queen Elizabeth I, King James I, Sir Walter Raleigh.

Letter of about 1608 from Robert Cecil to his son, Viscount Cranborne (Cecil Papers 228/22).

document itself. William and Robert Cecil must have had their own system of filing correspondence and probably arranged their letters in bundles or drawers. Sadly, this 'original order' of the collection has been lost as the manuscripts were bound largely in chronological order, which was only disregarded in the case of a few guard books, which were devoted entirely to particular groups of documents, such as royal letters, treaties, and genealogical papers. However, the early

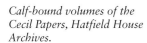

Calf-bound volumes of the Cecil Papers, Hatfield House Archives.

binding of the collection, which took place due to the recognition of the collection's importance and a desire to preserve it for future generations, has helped to protect the collection from deteriorating and individual manuscripts from going missing or being stolen.

The Cecil Papers have survived for over 400 years, largely in excellent condition and have made a monumental contribution to our understanding of the period of history to which they relate. Preservation and access are the two cornerstones of managing a collection of archives such as this and it is essential to achieve a balance between the two, whilst also being mindful of the fact that they are stored in a private family home. Handling a document will inevitably hasten its deterioration and poor storage conditions such as high humidity or changes in temperature can have an even more devastating effect on them. However, the value of the collection is in its use to those writing history, and as

Endorsement on a letter from Sir Thomas Fane to Sir Robert Cecil, 'Hast hast post hast hast hast for life life life', with a drawing of a gibbet (Cecil Papers 92/162)

such, scholars have always been allowed to have access to the material, whether in its original format or in one of the two microfilm copies of the collection. Since the 1970s, the Cecil Papers have been kept in a secure, fire resistant and climate controlled storage facility, only being brought out occasionally for research purposes or to be exhibited. A continuous preservation programme means that any deterioration has been reversed and the result is that the collection is in good condition and regularly used.

Early in 2010 we began the long process of digitising the Cecil Papers, which has had the twofold benefit of expanding access to the collection, by making it available to university students throughout the world, while discouraging non-essential handling of the original manuscripts. We installed an A1 scanner in a small room near to the archives, with which we could capture digital images of each of the 30,000 documents in the collection. A second scanner was soon added and it took two operators almost six months to complete the scanning of the bulk of the papers. At the same time, the calendar of the collection was also being digitised, which meant that each description could be linked to its corresponding document, making it easier for on-line users to locate documents relevant to their research.

Some documents, in particular some of the sixteenth century maps, were too large for the in-house scanner and had to be transported to an outside scanning unit for image capture. One of the greatest challenges during the project was the digitisation of the large pedigree of Queen Elizabeth I, which is displayed in between the Library and the top of the Adam and Eve staircase. The pedigree, which is made from vellum dates from the

Digitally photographing a section of Queen Elizabeth's pedigree in the Library at Hatfield.

A detail fom the parchment roll pedigree of 1559 tracing Queen Elizabeth I's ancestry back to Adam and Eve. The roll is about 22 yards long and this detail shows William the Conqueror on a horse.

sixteenth century, is 22 yards long, and has been glued into two wooden rolls and housed in a sealed cabinet. After taking the front off the cabinet and unrolling the pedigree, we realised that it would be impossible to remove it to be scanned off-site. A photographer came to the house to photograph the document in situ. It took an entire morning to unroll it and it had to be photographed in 47 sections due to its size. These images then had to be digitally 'stitched' together to put onto the on-line resource.

The library and archives at Hatfield House are administered full-time by two professionally-qualified archivists. The project to digitise the Cecil Papers shows a great commitment to preserving them and making them available for research and is the beginning of a new era in the management of the collections at Hatfield House. The digitisation of the Cecil Papers will ensure that they continue to be used as one of the most important sources of information for the Elizabethan and Jacobean periods.

Hatfield House as a Cultural Centre

DOUGLAS SLATER

WE THINK of country houses as a glorious aspect of our national heritage, but country houses were not built as cultural centres. They were built to display power, and to house the substantial numbers of people – family, guests, retinue, servants – that power attracts. Of course, art often formed part of the display. Usually this meant the visual arts, but from time to time, as at Hatfield, it included the performing arts, usually in the shape of house musicians. Robert Cecil kept his own band of musicians, as is discussed by Lynn Hulse elsewhere in this volume, and at the end of the eighteenth century the 1st Marchioness had a band that played regularly on the terrace on Sundays.

Fast forward to the present, when power has moved away from country houses, so that such displays have been for a century (give or take) an irrelevance and, indeed, an economic impossibility. Nowadays we conceive of art and culture as being for and about different things. Still, great houses have cultural gravity. They draw cultural activity to them. Sometimes such activity forms part of the demanding economics of their upkeep, as a way of attracting paying visitors. Sometimes the owners of a house generously make it available on occasion to local charities or societies to raise funds or otherwise promote their objects. Country houses tend to have large and often beautiful rooms and, if they are open to the public, the ancillary facilities for audiences – catering and loos – that underpin the highest of culture. All of this is certainly the case at Hatfield.

Where a house is still in private ownership, the culture that it attracts will tend to reflect its owners' interests. This is a form of cultural diversity that even the National Trust, for all its good work, cannot reproduce. Over the past seven years or so, Hatfield has become the home of the Hatfield Conferences on the Arts, marrying its own cultural gravity with its historic role as one of the great Tory houses. The Conferences began in 2004 as a means of re-connecting the Tory tradition with the arts and arts policy. There seemed then to have grown up a false sense that Toryism did not sufficiently value the arts and their contribution to the life of this country, and that a real and practical concern with fostering the arts could only come from the Left. The aim was to counter that wrong impression, and spread debate on arts policy across the political spectrum. The Conferences have never been narrowly partisan. Their guiding principle is that the arts are more important than politics.

If it is not too early to say so, the Conferences have now grown into a broad continuing conversation about arts policy, under Chatham House Rules, drawing people in and developing trains of thought that may be useful to those working in the arts, and to politicians in developing policy relating to the arts. There have been more than 25 of them since they began, some focussing on specific areas – for example orchestral music, theatre, the contemporary visual arts – and some on concerns across disciplines – for example, on education for the

Psappha, a group specializing in new music who are to play a new work by Ben Foskett commissioned by Lord and Lady Salisbury.

arts, and how central and local government develop and administer arts policy. They have also been concerned with the place of the arts in wider policy – for example, how the arts can assist in urban renewal.

For Hatfield's quatercentenary the aim is to celebrate its domestic musical tradition. In September 2011 two concerts are being held, with the same pro-gramme given twice, once in the Old Palace and once in the Marble Hall. One will reflect the music of 1611, and the other music of 2011. The former will be performed by Harry Christophers and The Sixteen, together with Fretwork, the outstanding modern viol consort. The latter will be performed by Psappha, a group specializing in new music, who will be celebrating their own 20th anniversary this year, and who will perform a new work by Ben Foskett, commissioned for the occasion by Lord and Lady Salisbury.

These will be by no means the first concerts given in recent years in either the Old Palace or the Marble Hall, but the hope is that they will be milestones towards a revival of Hatfield's musical tradition, both old and new, transmuting the house's latent cultural gravity into actual music-making of the highest standard. It deserves nothing less.

Harry Christophers and the Sixteen, who are to play a concert of early seventeenth century music at Hatfield as part of the 400th Anniversary celebrations.

Henry Moore in Hertfordshire

ANITA FELDMAN

Anita Feldman is Curator of 'Moore at Hatfield' and Head of Collections and Exhibitions, The Henry Moore Foundation.

HENRY MOORE is often viewed as a quintessentially English, specifically Yorkshire artist, yet he found an audience for his work worldwide and lived in rural Hertfordshire for over 45 years. Whilst there is no doubt that the craggy rock formations of the Yorkshire moors resonate through many of his sculptures, it is perhaps surprising that apart from his pre-war carvings, all of Moore's sculptures were created in Hertfordshire. He was an extremely prolific artist; more than 700 sculptures (excluding editions) were created within a cluster of intimate studios in the Hertfordshire hamlet of Perry Green, in addition to over 5,000 drawings and approximately 1,000 etchings and lithographs, each with numerous states and proofs. Even the Moore carvings hewn from the Italian marble quarries famously used by Michelangelo in the mountains above the town of Querceta began as small plaster maquettes at Perry Green, inspired by the shapes and forms of nature in the Hertfordshire landscape.

In this rich farmland, with medieval forests and sweeping open fields, Moore found a treasure trove of flints, animal bones and gnarled roots and branches that were the genesis of his sculptural forms. He collected these fastidiously for decades. The artist's Bourne Maquette Studio, named for the stream meandering through the hamlet, remains as it was during his lifetime. Here, clustered on shelves, the myriad shapes of found objects interspersed among the plaster forms of

man at various stages of completion, can appear both wondrous and strangely disconcerting. In these chance juxtapositions Moore discovers a landscape within the curvature of a bone and transforms the holes and points of flintstones into studies of the human form.

The Moore exhibition at Hatfield brings this concept to the fore. Close inspection of many of the seemingly abstract sculptures reveal their organic origins, such as the interlocking stones of *Locking Piece*, 1963–4; the pointed flint for *Torso*, 1967, and the seed pod that became the enigmatic *Large Totem Head*, 1968. *Relief No.1*, 1959 was created by pressing flints and other found objects into clay, casting the resulting impressions in plaster, and then creating a plaster enlargement from which the bronze edition was cast. As Moore's bronzes found homes throughout the world, so did resonances of the Hertfordshire landscape.

Moore and his wife Irina moved to Perry Green in September 1940. They had been visiting their friend, writer and politician Leonard Matters, near Much Hadham when their London home and studio suffered bomb damage during the Blitz. The Moores had already been forced to evacuate their cottage in Kent due to the threat of invasion. By chance, part of a sixteenth century farmhouse known as Hoglands was available for rent; over time the Moores were able to purchase the entire house and adjacent fields, now home to The Henry Moore Foundation. In a letter of November 1940 to

Moore standing beside the Top Studio and Hoglands in Perry Green, Hertfordshire, c. 1946.

Jane Clark, wife of his friend and patron Sir Kenneth Clark, Moore wrote:

We're here at a village in Much Hadham in Hertfordshire. Do you know this part? Its surprisingly pretty and unspoilt for being so near to London (27mls). I think we may stay here for some time . . . I've joined the Home Guard here and go out on night duty patrolling the country lanes twice a week.

The first traces of his new environment can be found in drawings as early as 1940. Apart from a few terracotta maquettes leading to the family groups and the Northampton *Madonna and Child*, 1943–4, sculpture production virtually ceased due to shortage of materials during the war. Even in compositions as early as 1940 Moore's ideas for sculptures are depicted sharing the

fields of Perry Green with local livestock. His powerful series of Shelter Drawings of Londoners in the Underground during the Blitz are broken by sudden juxtapositions of images of war infiltrating into the countryside around Perry Green, such as aircraft that have crashed into fields alongside grazing cattle. *Eighteen Ideas for War Drawings,* 1940 consists of a storyboard of annotated subjects for possible future drawings, with transcriptions including: 'flashes from ground'; 'gunshells bursting like stars'; 'disintegration of farm machine'; 'haystack & airplane'; 'burning cows'; 'barbed wire' and 'cows & bombers'. The contrast between the devastation engulfing London and the relative tranquillity of the surrounding countryside is also noted in some of these sketches. To create the Shelter Drawings, Moore made regular journeys into London from Much Hadham, ventured along various Underground lines – including Liverpool Street Station – which was still under construction, with rows of figures lying in the tunnels themselves. In this disturbing subterranean world he pencilled notes in a small sketchbook, to remind him of a scene, and once back in Perry Green he worked these into sketches and often larger compositions using wax crayon, watercolour, pen and ink and gouache. Moore had a very sculptural way of drawing, building up layers of media and then scraping it back, sometimes using a pallet knife, or emphasising the solidity of forms appearing out of the darkness with black ink.

Moore had enjoyed working in the open air since the 1920s, and the rural Hertfordshire environment provided not only inspirational found objects, but also the opportunity to work on a greater scale. Many of his seminal early public sculptures were created in his Top Studio (named for its location at the top of the estate closest to the house), previously a stable block and village shop (it is still not possible to buy a pint of milk or a newspaper anywhere in the hamlet). These include two family group sculptures donated to nearby post-war redevelopments: Barclay School in Stevenage and the town centre in Harlow. Another pivotal work, *King and Queen*, 1952–3, currently sited against the backdrop of

Henry Moore, Eighteen Ideas for War Drawings, 1940 (HMF 1553) pencil, wax crayon, coloured crayon, watercolour wash, pen and ink on cream medium-weight wove, 274 x 376 mm.

the home of Queen Elizabeth I at Hatfield, was created in the year of the coronation of Queen Elizabeth II. Its subject provides a strong connection with the tradition of British monarchy, while its distinctly modern forms herald an optimistic future for a war-torn Europe where public sculpture is intended to have an intrinsic role within the daily life of a community.

The ability of Moore's work to transcend a particular time and place and across many cultures is apparent in the unabated demand for his sculpture worldwide. Casts of *King and Queen*, as just one example, can be found in Oslo, Middelheim, London, New York and Los Angeles, as well as Dumfriesshire, Perry Green and Atami, Japan. Today the map of Moore 'Works in Public' on the Henry Moore Foundation website locates his sculptures in 38 countries. Likewise, both currently

ABOVE *Henry Moore, Reclining Figure: Angles, 1979 (LH 675) at Hatfield House, 2011.*

OPPOSITE *Henry Moore, King and Queen, 1952–53 (LH 350) at Hatfield House, 2011.*

and historically, Perry Green has been the destination of distinguished international visitors to see Moore's work in the surroundings in which it was created and in which he himself preferred – sited in the open air among sheep fields, gardens, meadows, orchards and woodland. Among the innumerable artists, architects, collectors, critics, dealers, writers, musicians and politicians to have visited Perry Green are Lauren Bacall, Peggy Guggenheim, Jo Hirshhorn, I. M. Pei, Mark Rothko, Barnett Newman, W. H. Auden, Billy Wilder, Somerset Maugham, Marino Marini, Joan Miró, François Mitterrand and Helmut Schmidt (who equated Moore's *Large Two Forms,* 1966 sited outside the former Federal Chancellery in Bonn with German reunification) and HM Queen Elizabeth The Queen Mother.

Yet despite this global artistic and intellectual network, Moore's work reveals a subtle and personal appreciation of the local topography. Pen and ink drawings of sheep in the surrounding fields, watercolour studies of cloud formations and etchings of the tangled roots and upraised branches of trees in nearby forests coincide with the creation of bronzes to be sited in landscape. Moore avidly drew bonfires in the fields, piles of logs in the forest, photographed the texture of bark. He experimented with collage and photography to work

out ideas for siting his sculpture in the landscape. Open fields appear in many studies, often as sites for reclining figures wherein the forms of landscape are echoed within the curves of the body and its drapery. The relationship of figure to landscape, man and environment is one that is becoming ever more important in the study of Moore's sculpture. The artist's questioning of this relationship can be clearly seen in works sited at Hatfield such as *Two Piece Reclining Figure No.2*, 1960 and *Reclining Figure: Angles*, 1979 – the former with its solid yet fragmented form and deeply textured surface evoking both the erosion and timelessness of archaeological ruins, and the latter through the figure's majestic and graceful sweeping curves echoing local hills and valleys.

Exhibitions of Moore's outdoor sculpture such as this one in Hatfield are surprisingly rare, due to the costs and logistics involved in insurance, packing, transporting and installing monumental sculpture, as well as issues of security and availability of work. Apart from The Royal Botanic Gardens, Kew, in 2007 there has not been another major outdoor exhibition of Moore's work in the UK for over twenty years. The achievement of this project was due to the foresight of Lord and Lady Salisbury, who had the vision and determination to make possible not just this exhibition, but an ongoing outdoor sculpture programme for the gardens of Hatfield. The differences between the Kew and Hatfield installations are notable. The gardens at Kew are distinguished by their vast sight lines with avenues of stately trees and grand Victorian glasshouses.

In the grounds of Hatfield, however, the viewer's experience is surprisingly personal – one can explore arbours with seemingly secret inner gardens, and amble through meadows and woodland with bluebells and other wildflowers. The Hatfield selection was made specifically for this venue – each work carefully chosen and sited to relate to the surrounding foliage and historic architecture. Throughout the seasons, the relation-

Henry Moore, Mother and Child, 1949 (LH 269b) at Hatfield House, 2011.

ship of the sculptures to their surroundings also changes. The way the low light of autumn glows in the inner recesses of *Reclining Connected Forms*, 1969 or the reflections pooling on the base of *Three Piece Reclining Figure: Draped*, 1975 after a shower of rain, or an unexpected view through the trees enclosing *Hill Arches*, 1973, enhance one's experience of sculpture in the open air. All of Moore's major themes are present here: seated and reclining figures, mother and child; internal/external and interlocking forms. The works

Henry Moore, Draped Reclining Figure 1952–53 (LH 336) at Hatfield House, 2011.

span nearly forty years of artistic endeavour and reflect a remarkable variety of surface textures and treatments, from the lustrous green patina of *Mother and Child, 1949* to the smooth black *Reclining Figure: Arch Leg, 1969–70* or the brilliant white fibreglass *Large Reclining Figure, 1984*.

Moore's presence is still felt locally. The stone heads he carved in 1953 for the façade of St Andrew's Church in Much Hadham are a reminder of his long-held interest in Romanesque and medieval carvings, whilst also bearing a regal outward gaze and fine delineation of fea-

Hoglands, Moore's home at Perry Green, where he lived for over 40 years with his wife Irina and daughter Mary. Today, the house and garden are open to the public and the 70 acre estate is the site of the Henry Moore Foundation

Henry Moore, Large Totem Head, 1968 (LH 577) at Hatfield House, 2011.

tures similar to *King and Queen*, cast in bronze the same year. A stained glass window created by Patrick Reyntiens from one of Moore's tree studies adorns its interior and was dedicated as a memorial to Moore in 1995. Following an elaborate service at Westminster Abbey in 1986, Moore was buried in the quiet and simple grounds of St Thomas's Church in Perry Green, joined by his wife Irina three years later.

Today The Henry Moore Foundation, established by the artist in 1977, looks after a world renowned collection of his work and makes this accessible through exhibitions and loans regionally and worldwide. The Foundation maintains the artist's home, studios and sculptures in the grounds at Perry Green much as they were in his lifetime, as well as a library and archive for research. Although open to the public, it remains a tranquil oasis, belying the flurry of sculptural production that once existed in this niche of rural Hertfordshire.

The Estate Today

PETER CLEGG

Peter Clegg was born in 1963 and grew up at Hatfield where his father Harry Clegg acted as Agent to the 6th Marquess of Salisbury. He trained as a Chartered Surveyor and worked in Property and Investment in Central London. In what has now become known as the 'family business' he returned to Hatfield as Chief Executive in 2001. He is married with three particularly nice teenage children.

My FATHER, Harry Clegg, helped to guide the Estate through the 1960s and 70s under the stewardship of the 5th and 6th Marquesses of Salisbury. I grew up on the Estate as a young boy, and like so many sons of successful fathers I determined not to follow in Harry's footsteps, but pursue what I perceived to be a more glamorous property career amongst the bright lights of London. It was therefore somewhat ironic that in November 2000 I should find myself in a state of some trepidation waiting to be interviewed by the 7th Marquess for precisely the role that I had sought to avoid for many years. He, on the other hand, was rather amused by the prospect of another Clegg 'having a go at Hatfield' and thoroughly approved of the hereditary principle being extended to the management team.

Coming back to Hatfield after an absence of some 20 or so years, and indeed breaking and entering without permission in order to have a look around and refamiliarise myself prior to that final interview, it was clear that much had changed. But much had not. The Park was still as I remembered it, littered with ancient oaks watching over the traditional landscape and blankets of daffodils defining the rides down to the Broadwater, interspersed with old buildings hidden away in forgotten corners quietly waiting to be called upon for a new role and some tender restoration.

This is perhaps one of the great challenges which

The Broadwater looking downstream towards the Red Bridge.

Robert, 6th Marquess of Salisbury.

Harry Clegg, Agent at Hatfield 1965–1982, and father of Peter Clegg, present Managing Director of Gascoyne Cecil Estates.

faces these wonderful old estates: to preserve their timelessness and great history whilst also encouraging them to evolve so that they remain relevant and can continue to play an important role in the local community. They must also earn their keep so that they remain intact for future generations to enjoy. For nothing is more certain than the onset of terminal decline if they are allowed simply to stand still, or if the preservation of the past outweighs any recognition of the needs of the present and the future.

In any event, if great estates and their historic buildings are not alive and vibrant, full of activity and laughter or debates of significance, what purpose do they serve?

Estates are often diverse places and Hatfield is no exception. It encompasses a large rural business from farms, both in-hand and let, to old woodlands. There is an extensive portfolio of built houses and commercially let properties as well as a complex visitor operation. This ranges from those who simply wish to visit the House, to those coming from afar to enjoy a concert, visit a country show, see their friends married or take advantage of the corporate hospitality offered in the Old Palace and Riding School. These various activities must all be taken into consideration without forgetting that it is also a home for the Cecil family.

The endless canvas of land and buildings that comprises the Estate has not altered dramatically over the decades. Of course, from time to time buildings have been rebuilt to replace those that have become derelict, and new trees or hedges planted where their predecessors have withered, but what is so remarkable is that this canvas allows successive generations to adapt it and react to differing demands of the age in which they live. Fields that only 30 years ago would have been filled with lush grass and grazing Friesian or Jersey cattle serving the dairy needs of the local community now grow cereal crops, peas, beans and oilseed rape for sale into a world commodity market.

Buildings which might have housed farm or forestry machinery, haylage, timber, ironsmiths and draughtsmen, are now restored to their former glory as offices, shops, school nurseries, or present day artisan workshops.

The survival of the Hatfield Estate depends on it being able to respond to the changing demands of the age, and adapting its various businesses to suit. It cannot operate successfully in a vacuum. To do this it must not only be aware of, and be responsive to, the various political, economic and social trends in the broader national context; it must also recognise that it forms an integral part of the prosperity of the local community. In short it must ensure that this community is a better place to live, work, and, socialise because of the presence of the Estate and activity generated by it.

Of course, the Hatfield locality has always benefited both directly and indirectly from the Estate because of its contribution to the local economy through employment, the buying and selling of materials, general goods and produce and the taxes that it pays. However, it does have to do much more than this and must take responsibility for and contribute to broader local issues such as education, the environment, charitable organisations and those who are less advantaged. A combination of all these things will allow the Hatfield Estate to survive and prosper.

Andres Duany, an American architect and town planner of Cuban origin, recently visited the Estate. He conducted what he calls a 'Charrette', a design workshop to which the local community contributes ideas, in respect of the village of Old Hatfield. The village has sadly declined over recent years through a combination of inappropriate 1970s development, a by-pass, and the development of Hatfield New Town. Many who still live in the Old Town, together with those on the Estate,

Hatfield Old Town Charrette: Andres Duany builds consensus.

remember it in its pomp and want to see it restored to its former vibrancy.

All locals were invited to the Duany Charrette, during which architects enabled those present to visualise the consequences of their contribution to the debate through sketches, plans and perspectives. Rather than the more normal approach to public consultation, which typically comprises a developer trying to impose a pre-conceived scheme on the unsuspecting local constituents, a Charrette involves everyone right from the beginning. At the end of some exhausting days for all concerned, plans emerged which have general support because of the inclusive nature of the process. We even asked local school children from the de Havilland Primary School what they thought – rather predictably they came up with some of the most obvious ideas which the professionals had missed.

It is always satisfying to be involved with school children of whatever age. The Estate runs a 'Living History' programme which tries to bring to life Tudor times at Hatfield with actors playing kings and queens and courtiers and by dressing up some of the old buildings. Similarly, on the rural side, the Estate runs a Country-side Foundation day where children meet farmers, a gamekeeper and foresters to see what they do. These days are important because they bring the Estate to life for the next generation in a way which is fun, hopefully sowing the seeds for some of the children to come back and visit or work with the Estate in the future. By understanding the Estate they gain respect for it and the diversity of life and activity that it encompasses.

All of these demands require the skills of a dedicated team, all of whom must understand the multitude of roles that the Estate may be juggling at a particular time. In attracting such individuals, Hatfield has indeed been very blessed over recent years.

Just today for example as I walk around the House and its surroundings, I encounter gardeners, foresters, property surveyors, land agents, conservation ladies, guides, event planners, farmers, the gamekeeper and many more. The variety of activity is extraordinary. One normally associates Joan Kendall's conservation team

Living History in the Long Gallery.

with the arts of intricate and painstaking needlework – but here they are laying out tapestries in the East Gardens to be washed. Around the corner in the deer park the forestry team are busy marking trees as part of our continuous cover programme and in the distance the building department are re-roofing Keepers Lodge. Where else could one find so much diversity within a half hour walk? It is all of these people that make Hatfield what it is, with their professionalism, enthusiasm and great desire to contribute to the Estate's present and future prosperity.

If one looked back some 20 or 30 years to my father's time, many of these roles would still have existed even if the emphasis on specific businesses was different. As technology has made great strides, farming, conservation and all other rural enterprises need far fewer people than they did then. For example, it would have been inconceivable to have imagined that two men with

However, all of these consultants and contractors gradually become friends of the Estate and grow to care deeply for it. In this sense, although the way in which we all work and are employed may change over time, the feeling of being a part of the Estate Family does not.

Having said this, it can feel somewhat surreal at times to be communicating with the outside world and colleagues from a seventeenth century bedroom via Blackberries, i-pads, and portable laptops, looking out over the deer park through a full-height stone-mullioned bay window. There is never an excuse for not being able to conduct a business transaction in such surroundings.

Running the Hatfield Estate has to be about achieving a balance – a balance between being commercial and profit driven in respect of some businesses and recognising that other areas require an altogether different approach. This balance will occur quite naturally provided that the Estate continues, as it always has done, to

An artist's impression of what the open area facing the North Front will soon look like. Compare this with the aerial photograph on page 53 showing it as a coach and car park. One of the strengths of Hatfield House is that it is constantly adapting to changing circumstances whilst at the same time preserving its history.

modern machinery could farm the Estate with just a student or two at harvest. The Clerk of Works team would have comprised buildings surveyors, architects, carpenters, bricklayers, plumbers, and electricians – all employed in-house. Today, much of this work is contracted out to third parties under only one of two project managers who remain directly employed.

Pepperpot Lodge, originally designed by John Donowell in about 1780 to reflect the Jacobean architecture of Hatfield House, is one example of the variety of house shapes and sizes to be found on the Estate.

OPPOSITE *Winter at Hatfield: a view of the House from New Pond.*

The view out over the park from Peter Clegg's office.

cultivate its friends and those who give so much of their time to work on it. It will be a source of great satisfaction to visit the Estate in future years when its guardianship is in the hands of others and to be able to recognise so many landscapes, buildings and chattels which will appear to be virtually unchanged at first glance but which may well be fully utilised in a role that differs almost completely from today. If that is the case, it will be a sign that the Estate is alive and vibrant as it adjusts again to changing times.

Earning Our Keep

NICK MOORHOUSE

Nick Moorhouse studied Classics at The University of Reading, and is married with a six-year-old daughter. Prior to taking up his current role in 2008 as Business Development Director at Hatfield House, he was employed by The Compass Group as the Managing Director of their exclusive divisions of Leith's and Payne & Gunter.

To MAINTAIN the House and Park at Hatfield costs a huge amount of money. In addition to the proverbial roof, there is the central heating and electricity, plumbing, running repairs, security, cleaning and showing of the public rooms, the garden, and the Park. It is a long list. My job, which I took on three years ago, is to generate enough business to help maintain the House and Park without causing damage to the House itself. It is a huge challenge, and one that has inspired a complete reorientation of the Park and how visitors will see it.

For decades, Hatfield has given a glorious day out to millions of visitors, their interests being particularly focused on access to the beautiful landscape of the Park, the famous garden, and of course the art and architecture of the House itself. Our success has been in no small part due to the wonderful team of mostly locally-based and dedicated guides within the House, some of whom have been with us for more than thirty years. The whole Estate has a policy of recruiting locally, running a successful apprentice scheme which in some cases has led to full-time employment. We also enjoy a consider-

The public queuing in the West Garden for the Antiques Road Show.

Fiona Bruce, presenter of the programme, with Lady Salisbury looking at a book from the library.

able amount of business from events on the Queen Elizabeth Oak Field, filming, catering, and money taken on the gate.

However, these methods of generating income are neither sufficient to fund the enormous expense of the upkeep of Hatfield, nor broad enough to satisfy the changing demands of the public. Neither do they help the increasing damage that the footfall of visitors does to the House, nor respect the requirements and privacy of the Salisbury family themselves, the staff who work on the Estate and the commercial and residential tenants. We needed a project that solved all these problems without sacrificing the fabric or reputation of the House itself. To this end, we are extending the Park's interest to the western part of the Estate.

'The West Side Story', as it has been affectionately named, hopes to do all this – to recognise the long-term financial opportunities of the House and the Park and appeal to visitors of all ages and backgrounds.

Our first challenge was to find a traffic route to, and build a car park on, the west side of the Estate. Planning permission was sought, a process which may sound simple on paper, but because of the historic importance of the House and Estate involves a considerable amount of uncertainty and dialogue with the local community and planning authority. Fortunately, permission was granted. The result is a brand new entrance – George's Gate – and two parking areas, the first of which opened in 2010 and the second in January 2011. This has enabled us to begin returning the North Front to its former, landscaped appearance.

George's Gate, named after George's Field, at whose north-western corner it sits, opens onto the Great North Road (A1000). We hope to encourage visitors to stay for the whole day rather than for what was normally two or three hours. With a view to this, we have restored a number of shops, significantly increased the capacity and range of food in the restaurant, built a wonderful adventure playground, and introduced a traditional breeds farm.

Up until 2010, we had a single gift shop. Since then, we have restored ten outbuildings to their former use as shops – from a plant nursery to antique and jewellery shops to an old-fashioned sweet shop, a great favourite with the younger visitors. The Stable Yard shops sit in a courtyard lain with granite setts, with a central fountain with a pineapple, symbolising hospitality, on its summit. The Hatfield House Gift Shop itself is very popular, stocking memorabilia of the House, Hatfield Park Farm, and the 2011 Moore at Hatfield exhibition.

The Coach House Restaurant was completely re-designed and refurbished during the winter of 2010, and now includes an open bakery. Customers will also be able to use the former small meeting room named the

The Old Palace awaits its guests.

Bloody Hollow: the new playground with the miniature replica of Hatfield House in the middle.

Cecil Room and a terraced area on the first floor above the restaurant. Our catering partner, Leiths, has invested considerable capital in the project, believing that there will be a far larger number of visitors since we will not simply open the shops and restaurant in Stable Yard between Easter and the end of September like we used to, but (excepting one winter month) for the entire year. The Old Palace and Riding School will continue to be hired for corporate and private events throughout the year. The Old Palace has been the home of the 'Hatfield Banquets' for the last 37 years. Hundreds of thousands

have enjoyed these Elizabethan-themed dinners with a company of actors creating a fun atmosphere by performing authentic period music among other things, for both private and corporate functions.

Whilst the restaurant and shops to the north of the new car park provide wonderful interest, to the west we have built a new adventure playground in Bloody Hollow, the central feature of which is a ten-foot high model of Hatfield House. The bespoke contents and apparatus within Bloody Hollow were built in Kings Lynn and shipped down by trailer during the summer of

White Park cattle arriving from Cranborne for Hatfield Park Farm.

2010. Bloody Hollow has been broadly acclaimed as one of the finest adventure playgrounds in the south of England.

The 7th Marquess is committed to the maintenance and development of stocks of traditional breed animals. As well as providing a further attraction to visitors, this has led to the creation of Hatfield Park Farm on the site of what used to be George's Field. The farm is stocked with dozens of traditional sheep such as Hebridean, cattle such as Long Horn, pigs such as Large Blacks and a fine collection of goats, ducks, turkeys, geese and chickens: all are on the rare breeds watch list.

We have taken on a knowledgeable young stockman, Tom Davis, to be responsible for their wellbeing, and are going to introduce a breeding programme, which will take place up the road from Hatfield Park Farm, at Home Farm, to assist the sustainability of traditional breeds indigenous to the United Kingdom. The livestock will be put out in unusually-shaped paddocks in George's Field, with walkways for the public between. The animals will be rotated to enable them to have some rest from the daily exposure to the general public. We will also introduce a tractor and trailer ride around the perimeter of Hatfield Park Farm, which will allow visitors, including the young and less able, to see the entire field.

The West Side Story should not be seen in isolation. It is part of a larger project, perhaps taking many years to come to fruition, which will see the town of Old Hatfield regenerated and joined with the Park to create a thriving community. This, broader, idea was borne out of the 'Charette' led by Andres Duany in 2008, described in the previous chapter.

We hope that in 2013 the offices that are currently based in the west wing of Hatfield House will be relocated to a new estate office in a walled garden to the south-west of the House. The current offices will be replaced by a new museum which will feature the skills required to run an estate such as Hatfield over the last 400 years, whilst demonstrating how these practices have changed. It will include displays of chattels, textiles, literature, pictures and paintings, and our own copy of the Cecil Papers.

Lord Salisbury with his Tamworth pig Judy, Interbreed Champion at Hatfield Country Show, 2009

OPPOSITE *Three views of the Hatfield Country Show: picnics on the showground, the Dancing Sheep, and heavy horses in the main ring.*

Filming 'V for Vendetta' outside the South Front. The film, set in a futuristic Britain, starred Natalie Portman, Stephen Rea and Hugo Weaving.

still captivates young and old. We shall also introduce a concert series both in the Old Palace and Riding School, and, on a larger and more popular scale, the Queen Elizabeth Oak Field. For many years, the Old Palace has also been the venue for our 'Living History' series, a programme that involves 10,000 children every year from across the county as part of their curriculum. In a day-long event, the children are taught how the Tudors lived and worked, are given some time in the Park, at the farm, and in the playground and leave with an educational as well as a rounded experience of the Old Palace, Hatfield and its history.

The creation of the West Side Story has combined the skills and knowledge of many colleagues who work in all departments, from the Forestry and Farm to the Archives and Hospitality, not least the support and commitment of Lord and Lady Salisbury. I am sure that this great project will be an enormous success in years to come, and perhaps act as a springboard for even greater success after our sensational 400th Anniversary celebrations.

In the past, academics and those with a specialised interest have been granted access to these important historical documents, but we have long been aware of the increasing number of institutions eager for a similar opportunity. Accordingly, we have digitalised the Papers, which will enable Hatfield to gain a new source of revenue and allow a broader audience to enjoy them.

Hatfield Park is renowned for its events, and we will continue to develop these over the forthcoming years. The Hatfield House Country Show in August has proven to be enormously successful and manages to combine the rural aspects of running an estate as well as giving families of all ages a wonderful day out with animals, arena events and shopping. Our craft event, 'Living Crafts', has been located here for nearly 40 years and despite changing habits and the advent of computers,

Fundraising for the Conservative Party: David and Samantha Cameron in the Long Gallery with Lord and Lady Salisbury and Viscount Cranborne (photograph: Antoinette Eugster).

House Guides

'It must be wonderful to be here as a guide', is a comment often made by visitors. The guides at Hatfield House have played an important role since the House was first opened to the public in 1948. Each year before the House opens, they meet and familiarize themselves with the history and absorb any changes that have taken place during the closed season.

Mrs Dorothy Craggs remembers being interviewed to become a guide in the early nineties. 'This involved an interview with Barbara Walton, the Assistant Curator. It felt exactly like entering a headmistress's study. Barbara Walton was a tall, formidable and commanding figure, but also kind and gentle. I admitted my knowledge was limited, but she didn't consider this a problem "as knowledge could always be acquired". So that was that and I became a guide in 1993.'

VISITORS' COMMENTS

Before climbing the grand staircase: 'They should have put in an escalator when the house was built.'

After visiting the library: 'Where does one buy a library ticket?'

An eight year old boy studying the Rainbow portrait of Elizabeth I with the large ruff: 'It occurs to me that Elizabeth had no neck.'

Guides' Works Outing: trip to Hever Castle, 2009.

Two young boys gazing at the portraits of Burghley and Robert Cecil holding their wands of office: 'They must be off to play snooker.'

Of an eighteenth century oriental cabinet of undecided origin, a visitor piped up, 'I know, because I have one at home, exactly the same, and mine is better than yours.'

An American visitor on hearing about the ice house was heard to say to her daughter, 'Darling, that's where they kept all the refrigerators in those days.

Conservation and Building

ANTHONY DOWNS

*Anthony Downs is Head of Building & Development at Gascoyne
Cecil Estates and is responsible for a team overseeing all building
work, conservation, planning and new developments. He studied
Building Surveying in Cambridge, gaining experience on a variety of
projects prior to joining Gascoyne Cecil Estates in 2000.*

Anybody visiting Hatfield Park in 2000 would have
been faced with a very different picture from the
one that greets them today. Like many other estates at
the start of the new millennium, Hatfield was faced with
changing circumstances. There were numerous redundant buildings and others in poor repair, yielding low
rents.

It was against this backdrop that I began work at
Hatfield in the spring of 2000. My initial brief was to
assess the condition of the built portfolio, establish a
thorough programme of refurbishment and maintenance,
whilst seeking fresh uses for many of the redundant
buildings.

The portfolio encompasses a wide spectrum of properties of almost every age, shape and size – ranging from
modern housing on the edge of Hatfield town to the
Tudor remains of the Old Palace. The variety and scale
of the problems we faced was almost as diverse. This
challenge filled me with a mixture of emotions – partly
daunted but full of enthusiasm.

It is always important to understand the spirit of an
estate like Hatfield. Whilst it is essential to keep one eye
on the future, one must never forget that it is first and
foremost a family home. It is also steeped in history and
has many traditions. Some of the latter are charming
and worthy of preservation. I am pleased to add that
some of the more dubious examples have been discon-
tinued. If organisations cannot adapt to changing
circumstances, they will die.

I have a long-held passion for architecture, construction and conservation. I believe that old buildings are
best preserved when sympathetically adapted to enable
them to remain in use and earning an income. The
challenge that faced us was which buildings should be
tackled first, which uses were suited to them, and how
could we procure the necessary consents and undertake
the physical work.

The first property chosen for conversion was Munns
Farm, located on the fringes of the Estate at Cole Green.
It comprised a derelict collection of farm buildings and
an uninhabited, listed farmhouse. We were successful in
gaining planning consent for a sympathetic conversion
of the farm buildings to office accommodation. The
work was done by teams of sub-contractors, many of
them local and self-employed. Although many lessons
were learnt – for we were dipping our toes into new
and uncharted waters – the building was successfully let
to a computer software company. Munns Farm provided confidence in the concept of rural offices at Hatfield and safeguarded a return on the initial investment.

Once the first phase had been completed, we turned
our attention to Munns Farmhouse, with the result that
in a little over eighteen months a completely derelict site
was transformed to an income-producing asset. The
buildings were once again in good repair and their
future safeguarded.

OPPOSITE *The fountain in Stable Yard.*

In the ten years since, the principles established at Munns Farm have provided the model for the successful refurbishment of countless other sites and buildings. Amongst them was a collection of largely derelict buildings at the very heart of Hatfield Park. Known as Home Yard and the Melon Ground, it was originally home to the traditional trades commonly associated with a large country estate – especially in its Victorian heyday. There were stables and garages, workshops for carpenters and plumbers, stores and a forge. The outbreak of the First World War in 1914 thinned the ranks of those who worked on the Estate, after which changing economic and social circumstances permanently reduced their number – making many of the buildings they worked in redundant. A further group of buildings dated back to the heyday of technological self sufficiency when Hatfield generated its own electricity. These too lay empty and in need of regeneration.

One cottage was so derelict that a tree was growing in it. Once that had been removed, the walls were partially rebuilt prior to the addition of a completely new roof that followed the pattern and form of the decayed original. Today the restored Whitesmiths Cottage is let as an attractive three bedroom home.

TOP *Munns Farm timber barn while restoration was in progress.*

BELOW *Munns Farm timber barn, following thorough refurbishment of a once derelict building.*

RIGHT *The old Team Stables, formerly occupied by the Forestry Department, photographed before the Melon Ground was redeveloped.*

The Melon Ground after rebuilding was completed in 2006.

Whitesmiths Cottage in derelict condition.

Whitesmiths Cottage after rebuilding, with a new slate roof in the style of the original.

The neighbouring cart lodge (now known as Wood-mans) was similarly close to the point of collapse. Wherever possible in its restoration, original materials were carefully salvaged and re-used. Where part was so decayed as to require partial dismantling, the details were carefully recorded first. We always try and retain original roof trusses, but in cases of severe rot or infestation green oak replacements are sourced from the Estate or local sawmills. Forestry has always played an important role at Hatfield, and we are lucky in usually being able to obtain what we need, be it a new truss or merely ash dowels for helping peg joints on new timbers.

This pattern of refurbishment was repeated over the next three years until all the buildings around the Melon Ground had been reborn as a series of eclectic business units. Today the signs outside their doors list everything from recruitment companies to private health advisers, toy importers to graphic designers. Once again the buildings are home to an active working community.

Having brought the Melon Ground back to life, our

The Building and Development office in Carters Row, newly constructed in 2006.

thoughts turned to the large scar created in the 1970s by the demolition of a further block of stables and workshops. Would it, we wondered, be possible to build new offices there, thereby restoring the form and massing of the area, creating what is known today as Carters Row? We were fortunate in that we possessed a collection of photographs clearly showing what had once stood there. Whilst they are not a slavish recreation, it was possible to design the new buildings in the spirit of their predecessors. The local planners were sympathetic to our approach, underlining how fortunate we are to enjoy a consistently good working relationship with Welwyn Hatfield Borough Council. Formal Planning Consent was granted in 2005.

Great care was taken over the selection of bricks and tiles, with gables stepped in sympathy with their neighbours and windows and doors chosen to reflect the vernacular traditon of the Estate. Internally the offices feature oak roof trusses and are generously lit by overhead conservation roof-lights. This, however, was not an exercise aimed at recreating a historic range of stables and workshops. We were of course seeking to create modern, if characterful, offices and the partial adoption of a structural steel frame allowed us to achieve generous clear spans and cantilevered mezzanine floors. Despite their traditional exteriors the units incorporate lifts, underfloor heating, extensive IT cabling and modern high efficiency office lighting.

As a bonus for our new tenants, an adjacent walled garden, which by 2002 had become the archetypal jungle, was carefully cleared and re-landscaped for their enjoyment. To date the Estate has created in excess of 50,000 square feet of office space in previously redundant buildings.

There is, of course, much more to Hatfield Park Estate than its commercial portfolio. Hatfield has long provided a venue for dinners, conferences and wedding receptions in the Old Palace and the Riding School.

By 2005 the Riding School needed a makeover. Built in the nineteenth century as an indoor riding arena, the building had not seen a horse since the 1950s. Since then it had seen service as a barn, a home for historic

vehicles, and as a venue for dining and conferences. Our intention now was to create a high quality, multi-purpose facility for everything from wedding receptions and conferences to meetings and product launches. Construction commenced in November 2005 with an enforced deadline of July 2006. Such was their optimisim, our corporate hospitality team had already enthusiastically let the building for a summer wedding.

From a careful survey of the brickwork, roof, and historic photographs it was obvious that the building was originally top lit by a clerestory lantern light that at some point in the past had been removed, leaving the interior devoid of natural light. We determined to replace the lantern light, doing so by commissioning moulded aluminium glazing bar sections. Internally, the height allowed the inclusion of galleries linking the two ends which we suspended from the original roof trusses. Fully-glazed balustrading lends the building a distinctly contemporary feel in contrast to the traditional, heavily timbered Old Palace.

Excavation of the floor also allowed the incorporation of underfloor heating served by a new subterranean plant room which also heats the Old Palace – though in the case of the Riding School the heating costs are substantially reduced by the generous use of high quality

ABOVE LEFT *The Victorian Riding School, as it looked in the 1960s.*
ABOVE *The Riding School in 2006, with the clerestory roof reconstructed in aluminium. It is now ideally suited for conferences, weddings and Estate parties.*

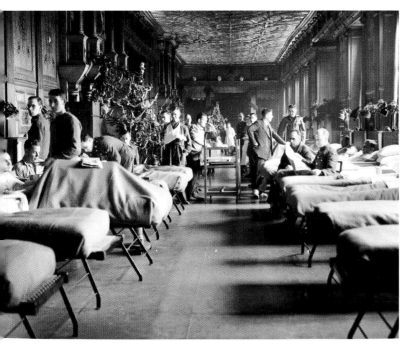

Two views of a wartime Christmas: patients in the King James's Drawing Room and the Long Gallery. Hatfield House was used by the Royal Army Medical Corps as a military hospital between 1939 and 1945.

insulation. As is necessary these days, the building includes a fully integrated Audio Visual system.

Throughout the period we were working on the Riding School, a parallel programme of repairs was taking place elsewhere. Cottages, town houses and flats were treated to reroofing, structural repair and in many cases full refurbishment. Wherever possible, inappropriate alterations were corrected and period details restored or reinstated.

As with the buildings on the Estate, so also with the ancient house as its centre. Hatfield House was occupied by the Army during the Second World War when it served as a military hospital. During the period of post war austerity the House was not immune to the national shortage of building materials. The love of hardboard, asbestos and a propensity to make do and mend or cosmetically cover over potentially bigger problems was perpetuated here, as elsewhere.

Fortunately the 5th and 6th Marquesses had the confidence and vision to oversee a thorough programme of external works, thus ensuring that re-cladding of the roof and extensive repairs to stone masonry were undertaken before more serious problems prevailed. The House has generally been well maintained and kept in good weather-tight order. It continues to benefit from being a living, breathing family home, a point made clear when visiting some of the more anodyne examples of historic country houses which have been reduced to the status of cold, empty museums.

One of the last wishes of the 6th Marquess was to see the restoration of the cupola roofs on the four garden houses which so complement the South Front. Sadly finished after his death, it was a pleasure to see the late Marquess's wishes honoured when, in time, the work was duly completed. Looking through the photographs we took at the time reminds me of the difficulties that freak weather conditions can occasionally play during such operations. A crane had been booked to lower the new cupolas into place. A late snowfall just prior to Easter made it a chilly task. The roofs were subsequently

OPPOSITE *Restoration of lead roofs on the South Front garden houses.*

Sections of the boilers, which were over 50 years old, being removed from the House in 2004 when the central heating system was renewed.

boarded in a traditional manner prior to the application of sand-cast leadwork. Finally, weathervanes echoing the design of those on the House were added to their summits.

The most complex – and costly – recent task has been the modernising of the central heating and the rewiring of a substantial part of the House. The 50-year-old boilers had been converted from oil to gas, and their performance was at best erratic. More worryingly, there were numerous old water tanks on the roof, adding considerably to its weight, and the consequences should any of them have burst or sprung a leak did not bear thinking about. The supply of hot water was similarly antiquated, depending on a series of elderly belt-driven, wheezing pumps. Basically, the entire system was obsolete. We had little option but to start again with a clean sheet.

Replumbing is always traumatic. To undertake it on a property as old and sprawling as Hatfield with its 20 bathrooms was a truly massive undertaking. After a feasibility study, we looked at various alternative technologies before concluding that a properly controlled system of gas boilers and water heaters offered the best balance between technical risk, capital cost and operating efficiency.

Ultimately it was agreed that we needed two plant rooms in the basement – one dedicated to heating, the other to hot water. The installation of their equipment was the easy part of the operation. Much more complex was routing the pipework through and around the House. Because of the historic importance of the House and so many of its contents, every single object in all the principal rooms was painstakingly photographed and recorded. Every painting was taken down and placed in a specially made wooden case. Finally everything – be it a teapot or four poster bed – was removed from the House and placed in two temperature-controlled pantechnicons. The final scheme, from start to finish, took the best part of a year and included the installation of some 4,500 yards of new copper pipework. Supervision of the small army of plumbers and electricians was, to say the least, a challenge. We had to be on a constant guard against damage by carelessness or attempts at shortcuts. In order to combat the risk of fire, a system of crimped copper joints was employed to remove the need for use of a naked flame.

One benefit of the replumbing and rewiring was an opportunity to make good previous unsatisfactory repairs, and reinstate the building fabric in a more careful manner. It is a tribute to the skills of the craftsmen who put the House back into good order after the work was finished, that it is difficult to guess the extent of opening up and general disturbance which was undertaken during this exercise. Today, the House is safe, warm and comfortable. When you turn on a hot tap, it is no longer necessary to wait for minutes on end for water more likely to be tepid than hot.

Before 2006 there were no state bedrooms on show. One outcome of the replumbing was the chance to convert the old billiard room into a new bedroom whose walls were then covered with hand-painted Chinese wallpaper. Now known as the Chinese Bedroom, a suitable bed was installed and the plaster ceiling incorporating the family coats of arms carefully repaired.

As part of the celebrations to mark the 400th anniversary we intend to complete the conservation of the ceiling of the Grand Staircase and the wall paintings and

ABOVE *Conservation work in progress on the ceiling of the Grand Staircase in 2011.*

LEFT *The Chinese Bedroom, decorated with hand-painted wallpaper, first opened to the public in 2007.*

A crane lifts one of the newly-restored weathervanes back into position on top of one of the South Front turrets, December 2010. Freshly covered in gold leaf, these vanes now glint brilliantly in the sunshine.

decoration in the Marble Hall. Restoration is also taking place in the Chapel.

Nor has the outside been ignored. A good example is the nine months spent on the recent restoration of the four weathervanes which crown the turrets on the South Front. The vanes and their associated spheres, finials and scrolls have all been repaired. After long exposure to the elements, the metalwork was severely corroded and fragile. The main shafts have been replaced in stainless steel and the spheres, scrolls and weathervanes skilfully repaired by G.D. Armitage (Clock and Belfry Work) Ltd of Market Harborough prior to the application of new gold leaf. In addition to the weathervanes,

one of the cupola roofs on the East Wing was found to be decayed. Once again the need to avoid the risk of fire led to the upper section of roof being carefully reconstructed in a local workshop, before being recovered in sand-cast lead and craned into position as part of a nail-biting, precision operation.

Hatfield is enriched by its history, but it cannot ignore the future. Today the Estate is using alternative technologies for heating – including biomass, ground and air source heating. We are looking at micro-hydro electric generation at a former watermill and other ways in which the Estate can contribute to energy generation. The work of the building team now extends beyond the immediate Estate boundaries and we are actively involved in the redevelopment of Old Hatfield and some areas within outlying villages. Alongside our traditional role as custodians of the buildings on the Estate, we are now in a position to be able to widen our vision by encouraging further sympathetic development, ensuring high standards of design and construction and paying close attention to detail – the very qualities that have enabled Hatfield House to endure for the last 400 years.

Dunhams Mews: the first phase of this new development in Old Hatfield was completed in 2010.

The Rural Estate

GAVIN FAUVEL

*Gavin Fauvel is Agent at the family's Cranborne Estate in Dorset and is
responsible for the Rural Estate at Hatfield. He trained at Seale-Hayne
Agricultural College in Devon and worked on a large estate in Cornwall,
qualifying there as a Chartered Rural Surveyor, before moving to Hatfield.
He is married with three young daughters.*

IF YOU LOOK on a map, Hatfield Park is an expanse
of green surrounded by motorways and railways – the
M25 to the south, the A1M to the west, the East Coast
Mainline, which skirts half the Estate, and a commuter
line to Cambridge – only 25 miles from London. The
Estate has always profited from trading routes going
north from, and its proximity to, the capital. As well as
being close to the huge market of London, it was the
first main staging post on the Great North Road – there
were about 20 pubs up Fore Street in the nineteenth
century. It also has, much more than might be said of a
strictly rural part of the country, been privy to a diverse
range of new people – some passing through, some
staying – but always bringing with them new energy,
ideas and approaches. By the very dint of living on the
urban fringe, the rural Estate at Hatfield has been accustomed to change: one could indeed argue that these
changes have been its life-blood.

To write about the shift in land-use at Hatfield since
1611 would take us from the feudal system of land
tenure, through the agricultural revolution, to 'Dig-for-
Victory', followed by the post war agricultural boom,
right to this modern age of satellite-steered tractors and
food being flown all around the globe in a consumer-
driven marketplace, one that sees the distinction in
seasonal product-supply markets removed.

Ever since the nineteenth century industrialists built
their factories (and the towns that grew with them) and
people left the land to go to work in them, there has

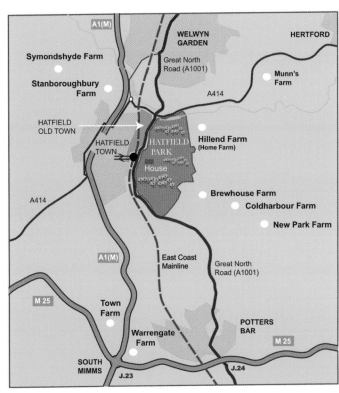

*A simple map showing the position of the main tenant farms, and the
way in which Hatfield Park is a green oasis surrounded by roads and
railways.*

been ever greater pressure to mechanise farming,
improve plant and animal genetics, and to feed the increasingly urban population. All these pressures are as
applicable today as they were then – possibly more so.

ABOVE *Fore Street, Old Hatfield, in about 1900.*

BELOW *Despite the impact of the changes of the twentieth and twenty-first centuries Old Hatfield retains much of its Georgian charm – as here, looking down Fore Street, with Goodrich House on the right.*

The Cecils have not been noted for their turnips or livestock improvement (although the present Lord Salisbury might disagree in the matter of pig-keeping and preserving old breeds), preferring instead to lend their energies (some generations somewhat significantly) to politics and the great affairs of state. They have, nonetheless, been strong stewards of their estates – encouraging progressive farming and good relations with tenants whilst also not being afraid to farm themselves.

Today, Hatfield has six main farm tenants who manage between about 300 and 600 acres apiece in areas located across the Estate from west of Stanborough, where Daniel Mackay farms at Symondshyde, to near Hertford, where Robert Shambrook farms at New Park Farm. Agriculturally, the land is not top-grade, being heavy, prone to drought, and gravelly – so much so that substantial deposits of sand and gravel are being extracted from Symondshyde. What was traditional dairy country has been steadily turned over to cereals, and, increasingly, livery yards – indeed, with the exception of Jeremy Waddup at Coldharbour Farm to the east of the Estate, all the tenants have added to their businesses, mostly with horses and sub-lets. The tenanted farms are very much a family affair: all have run their farms for at least two generations, with many members of each family helping. At Stanboroughbury Farm to the west of the Park, Peter Crawford and his wife Paula and their children are all actively involved; three generations of Whites live and work at Warrengate Farm, growing cereal crops and running a contracting business; at Brewhouse Farm in Wildhill, their cousin David Craig farms with his brother Dougal and son Stuart.

The MacKays, Crawfords and Craigs are all of Scottish descent. Many farmers here have Celtic origins, for, disappointed with the low-standard of farming in Hertfordshire, the 3rd Marquess advertised in Ayrshire towards the end of the nineteenth century for their reputedly talented farmers to take up tenancies further south where they would have access to the London milk market.

It is only recently that agriculture began to embrace renewed innovation. The final ten years of the last mil-

Warrengate Farmhouse, rebuilt in 2009.

lennium and the first few of this saw a decline in real incomes from farming. It has certainly been true of the Estate rent roll at Hatfield. Thirty years ago, farming rents and income would have made up some 80 per cent of total income. Changes to housing legislation and an increasing willingness to spend money on improving the Estate housing stock has shifted that balance, so that now farming incomes are less than ten per cent of the whole. They have not declined per se, just remained static whilst residential and commercial income has rapidly increased.

As we look to the next fifty years, the prospects for farmers are good. The population is growing faster than the land can sustain. More food is required, and increasing demand is being placed on the land to provide crops for fuel and clothing. Those who study population growth and have a distinctly Malthusian view of such rapid expansions are worried. Access to land and water, as shown by China and some Middle Eastern states buying land in Africa to feed their home populations, will increasingly be crucial.

Hatfield, rarely amongst its peers, does not have a range of model farm buildings in the great sense of those built elsewhere in the late Victorian era. Home Farm in the Park at Hatfield is a modest affair. Its brick-built pigsties, cow stalls, and an older Dutch-barn are the only remains of what might have a been a more extensive, older range. There are two rather more modern buildings – legacies of a grand age of dairying at Hatfield during the 1970s and 1980s under the 6th Marquess. He had dairies at Home Farm, Park Dairy and Hill End and would be a regular visitor at Home Farm – taking a short-cut across the South Front on foot to catch milking-time.

The hum of the vacuum pump and lingering smell of silage and slurry are no longer evident at any of the farms at Hatfield. The Craigs milked at Woodside up until ten years ago, deciding quite reasonably that running an up-market bed-and-breakfast for horses was more lucrative, especially with a ready market on the doorstep. It no longer seems possible to milk cows, for a half-decent profit anyhow, unless the herd is at least 500

Brewhouse Farmhouse. During the Second World War the white clapboard house was painted khaki so as to not to offer too visible a landmark to enemy aircraft bombing the nearby de Havilland Aircraft Factory, builders of the Mosquito.

Fallow buck in winter.

cows strong and uses the least amount of labour and inputs for the most amount of milk yield per cow.

These buildings now exist to support other enterprises on the Estate. Hill End farm buildings can store nearly 3,500 tonnes of grain and houses a grain drier and small workshop. The rest of the buildings here are now let for commercial warehousing. At Park Dairy, the buildings house spare materials, bricks, stone, roofing tiles and all sorts of interesting architectural flotsam, salvaged and stored for future use. It is also home to the Forestry Department.

Home Farm is being converted, once more, to house animals for the new rare breed farm, opening as part of the 400 year anniversary celebrations of Hatfield Park. It is not a commercial, but an educational farm, where we hope to engage and entertain visitors to the Park. One suspects that the short-cut across the South Front will once again be put to use by the 7th Marquess.

Hill End Farm is now the modern 'home farm' for Hatfield. The arable land here and within the Park at Park Dairy and remnant land of Home Farm is run as one unit, together with land at Munns Farm some few miles to the east. The farm is run in-hand and managed day-to-day by Daniel Mackay. The farm, despite being well over a 1,000 acres, supports two men on a part-time basis with the minimum of ultra-modern equipment.

Increasingly, conservation and shooting go hand-in-hand. The practice of vermin control, encouraging and planting wildflower seed and feed-seed mixtures, and taking care of hedges are now recognised as essential for farmland birds and wildlife, as well as for game birds. A single keeper keeps the in-hand shoot at Hatfield, providing five or six informal days of driven shooting for the family. In recent times, the shoot in the Park was let to a syndicate which released over 30,000 birds and shot twice a week from September to January. Happily, this has now stopped. Having a keeper who spends most of his time trying to get the balance of nature right is infinitely preferable to the kind of disruption wrought on the Park eco-system by the previous regime of 'put-and-take' keepering.

Queen Elizabeth I and others enjoyed hunting deer at Hatfield well before the Cecils arrived. In 2011, there are still the genetic remnants of the red deer that were hunted then. A small herd of about ten reds – hinds and a stag – are seen regularly between Pepperpot Lodge, Park Dairy, the Bushes and the Warren. Whatever the hazards they face elsewhere, they are neither shot nor hunted whilst in the Park, and seem naturally to keep to a sustainable-sized herd. A formal deer park was re-enclosed in 1996 and specimen fallow deer imported to create a new park close to the House. These deer are managed as for any proper closed-herd by annual culling and periodic importation of new genetics. The venison is sold locally to game dealers.

The Russell family has quite a bit to answer for in terms of the third species of deer – muntjac – that exists at Hatfield – it was from Woburn that they first escaped after the First World War. Muntjac breed all year and are difficult to see and control but, being about the size of a Labrador, are the perfect height to eat the shoots of young trees. The meat, making good eating, is small consolation. The spread of the original, now feral, escapees from the formal park at Woburn is unrelenting, with muntjac in evidence now as far as Devon and South Yorkshire. The considerable efforts being made to encourage the natural regeneration of the woods at Hatfield relies on ever-vigilant control of them through stalking.

Hunting with dogs is no longer legal, although the hunt continues to run across Hatfield. Before the ban, their quarry was already increasingly urbanised. The foxes of south Hertfordshire are more accustomed to raiding domestic rubbish bins than the hen-house and are seen more often in the gardens and back streets of the town than in open countryside. There is a well-attended Lawn Meet on the South Front at Hatfield every spring. To the uninitiated, it must seem odd that a field-sport that was so vociferously banned is apparently anything other than in decline.

To return to the map. Visually, the Estate looks more or less the same as it did a few hundred years ago. The boundary fences are in the same place; the lodges are still standing where they were originally erected; the House, the avenues and the lake are exactly as they were in 1611. However, the green fields to the east, to the north and to the south no longer exist. The town has come to the Park gate, as has the railway, the motorway, people and houses too. Their arrival has brought many changes to the Park – the land that once supported live-stock and many small farms now provides livery stables, places to work in converted farm buildings and some-where to walk dogs.

But amidst all this change, there is one important point of continuity, which always has and I hope always will exist at Hatfield – that the Estate and the town continue to coincide and support each other, making the other richer as a result. The generations of Cecils who are temporary stewards at Hatfield overlap with staff, buildings and land – all at different rates. They all, in their own way, revolve in a constant cycle. Those points of overlap provide stability, change and evolution in equal measure. That model of stewardship looks promising, for the next four hundred years, at least.

Farming Memories

FRANK LODGE AND HEINZ KUNTZE

Frank Lodge was born in 1929 in Ferrybridge in Yorkshire. He joined the Navy when he was 17 and left aged 25. He joined the farm staff at Hatfield and ended up as Arable Foreman. He retired in 1994.

I CAME TO Hatfield in March 1954 after spending eight years in the Royal Naval Air Service. I had come from a farming background, my father having his own farm in Yorkshire.

One of my earliest memories of my farming here was ploughing with a Ferguson tractor with no cab, sitting with my overcoat on and a railway sack over my knees to try and keep warm against the winter winds. We still got cold, so every so often we would stop and run up and down the headland to get the circulation going. We then got back on the tractor and carried on ploughing. We would repeat this all day. Farming at Hatfield in the '50s was on a small scale. The farm was 525 acres, running as far as Essendon Lodge and to the far end of Showground. We used small tractors and still had a reaper binder and a threshing drum. The corn was cut and stacked in the corner of the Showground field, and

we threshed it during the winter. It was then stored on the floor above the Forestry Shed which is now converted into offices. The Showground and Brimstone Hill areas were arable, and the rest was grassland used by the two dairies we had, Jerseys at Home Farm, and Ayrshires on Queen Elizabeth's Oak Field. Milking was done through a milking bale during the summer and at Park Dairy in the winter. They were still milked through the milking bale which stood on a strip of concrete and the cows lived in some old sheds. We also had a small beef herd of Black Pole and Aberdeen Angus.

It was not until the late '50s that we got our first combine harvester. We then geared up with larger tractors having taken more land in hand. It was about this time that farming took off in a big way.

In 1954 Old Hatfield was a thriving town with lots of shops and pubs. The Park was just opening to visitors on Saturdays and Sundays and Bank Holidays. I recall standing on the gate with a money bag over my shoulder and a roll of tickets.

There was only one tarmacadam road on the Estate, which was from the main gate, up the right hand side of the cricket pitch, up to, but not including, the House car park. All the other roads were of hoggin which we had to repair quite often. Tom Davis was head gardener in 1954. The house gardens had been neglected over the war years and still were in the '50s, but the walled garden was a going concern. It had underground irrigation and was growing a lot of vegetables and fruit. It supplied Hatfield House, the Lodge House and a shop, which was situated in the Old Palace. Dollimores, the local greengrocers, took any surplus. Next to the walled garden was the Pear Ground, where there were three big greenhouses, which were very productive. This is where most of the gardeners worked. The house garden was still neglected. This was in the 5th Marquess's time. He spent a lot of his time in government, so had very little time for the Estate and his main interest at Hatfield was forestry and shooting. It was not until the 6th Marquess came to Hatfield that the gardens began to change. He was and had been, while he was Lord Cranborne, interested in farming, hence the expansion of the farm at Hatfield. He also, along with Lady Salisbury, began to restore the House gardens and it was the time for the walled gardens to be run down.

Little else was done on the Estate. Farming was going strong and as Lord Salisbury did not have too much interest in the rest of the Estate, things were just kept ticking over in the other departments. The building department was kept busy on the outside properties and the houses were painted outside and inside and running repairs carried out. The forestry was kept quite busy planting, clearing and thinning. There were about 14–16 men employed on the forestry, Matthew McKendrick being the head forester.

During my time I worked for three Lord Salisburys, the 5th 6th and 7th. When I first came to Hatfield there were quite a few families that had spent their whole lives on the Estate. Some of them were very interesting such as Bill Mitchell aged seventy four, and Bill Norris who was eighty five. George Hemmings had worked for the 3rd and 4th Marquesses from when he was a 13 year old boy. He used to ride with the 3rd Marquess on his three-wheeled tricycle, then jumping off to push when he came to an incline. Les Hickson was the Clerk of the Works, with 16 men under him. He had been on the Estate from when he was 14 years old. He looked after the House during the war, when it was used as a hospital.

I recall once when we were fencing at the far side of the park, we came across these gates leading onto a bridle path. I learned later that the gates were numbered and had been installed for the 4th Marquess who was a keen horseman. He would come to a gate and, if he found it was difficult to open from his horse, he would make a note of it and report it to the office. There was, in my early days, a post on the other side of the road at the old estate office with a ring on it, where he would tie up his horse to go into the estate office. A pity it was pulled up. I think these sort of things should be preserved. The Marquess turned the Old Palace into stables, and it was here that the Duke of Wellington's last horse, a descendant of Copenhagen, was kept, and where he died and is buried. There is a plaque on the Old Palace wall. I showed it to my sister when she was on holiday, and she wanted to come down and clean it up. I put her off, telling her she would get me the sack.

A few years before I retired, whilst working up near Home Farm, I found a milestone laying on the edge of the road, buried with soil. I dug it out, and stood it upright, but I saw quite recently that it had gone. On another occasion, while mowing in Carter's Pond field in 1993, I came across a plaque which had been run over and broken. On it read: 'THIS TREE WAS PLANTED BY QUEEN VICTORIA IN 1846.' I gave it to the then under-agent, who said he would get it repaired and put back in its proper place. I never heard or saw anything of it again.

I can see that we have to move with the times and each one of the family make their mark on things, and rightly so, but I do think that some of these historic things should be preserved.

One of the brighter times was going out on day trips at weekends which were organised by Josie Jackson from the office. We sometimes went to the seaside, a show in London or a club in Watford. Much later on, in the '80s and early '90s we started to organise barn dances at Home Farm and square dances in the Riding School. We would decorate the walls and have straw bales for seats. These were a big success. It was hard work getting it all ready but well worth it. We also had Tramps Suppers and Fancy Dress Parties in the Estate Social Club.

Heinz Kuntze was born in 1925 in Leipzig, in what later became East Germany. He learnt to glide at the age of fourteen and is still gliding regularly off the Dunstable Heights. In 1946 he came to England as a Prisoner of War and worked for the Agricultural War Department (WARAG) in the workshop in Aylesbury. He married a beautiful English girl called Rose. Now on his own, he lives in the Park and keeps a Jowett Javelin his garage.

I CAME with my wife and son to Hatfield in 1958 having worked on a nearby estate in the same sort of work which could be described as agricultural engineering with variations.

To put it mildly, the workshop at Hatfield was not even basic: three adjoining sheds with corrugated tin roofs and dirt floors. Concrete was put down in one shed which had the front covered, and the other two were open to the elements. Workshop equipment was zero except for one electric welder.

As I had my own tools, I could function of a sort. Over a period conditions improved, a car lift was installed, and more equipment bought.

The reason for this primitive start was the Estate had no need for a workshop as farming was on a small scale. Gradually rented out farms were taken back in hand. Farming on a large scale started in the mid sixties with the acreage increasing to 2,300 acres. About 1000 acres were under cultivation and the rest was taken up by three dairy herds.

Having got the workshop to a satisfactory operation, the maintenance and repair of the equipment for the forestry, the gardens, the Clerk of the Works as well as all the cars was taken over. A few problems arose, one of which was the location of the workshop which could not take the large combines, tractors and other equipment, which of course had all increased in size. It was

decided to build a new Workshop and Implement Sheds in the Sawmill grounds. Having served a very sophisticated apprenticeship with the company Bussing NAG in Leipzig – Germany, now part of M.A.N. Germany, I knew what a good workshop should be like. The layout was left entirely to me and very much appreciated.

I made new solid work benches, the car lift was re-installed, an underground waste oil tank put in, which could be emptied by tanker, and space-heating installed. In the shed next door, an inspection and maintenance pit was dug, and a large lathe put in. The Workshop was light and airy.

Now what about the people who operated this sophisticated equipment which came in after World War II? Well, they coped extremely well, being thrown into this 'suck it and see' situation from a horse drawn era. Things have changed since then, especially now with electronics, computers, modern technology, and GPS coming into the equation. Proper training would also be necessary.

Although the majority coming to work on the farm managed very well, accidents and mishaps occurred, and occasionally irresponsible behaviour took place. I remember three incidents which seem amusing now, but could have had serious consequences. Before I mention what happened, I would like to talk about a very sloppy habit which had crept in with one or two tractor drivers, namely leaving the two brake pedals of the tractor unlocked. These brake pedals are normally locked together, but could sometimes be used independently. They had to be firmly locked together for road use. Incident one took place when the tractor driver was travelling at speed on the road when he had to make an emergency stop. This resulted in the tractor making a hundred and eighty degree turn, joining the oncoming traffic. I imagine the motorist saw all his past life flash before him, when all of a sudden, a tractor appeared in front of him. The cry went up: 'Brake Failure' and when the tractor came into the workshop with the brake pedals firmly locked together, no fault with the brakes could be found. The second incident was similar: the tractor was towing a ten ton trailer with cereals and

Heinz Kuntze combining in the 1970s.

remember hearing about occurred before I arrived at Hatfield, and was a story that went round all the tractor dealerships in Hertfordshire. A tractor was sent to the local dealer with a totally seized engine. It was repaired and returned to the farm. Not much later it happened again so they sent someone over to investigate. The driver was asked what sort of oil he used for topping up the engine, and he showed him a barrel filled with molasses. Now sugary substances don't do an engine any good at all.

Farming carried on at Hatfield until 1989 when the whole enterprise was shut down. There were several reasons: over-production, low prices, the cereal and butter mountains which were an embarrassment, and set aside had arrived. Where are the cereal and butter mountains now? Better not ask, people might get worried, I understand reserves are low.

I hope that the powers that be realize farming cannot be turned on and off like a tap. I doubt it.

During Heinz's time at Hatfield he regularly serviced all the farm vehicles including 7 Ford tractors, 2 Ferguson Tef tractors, 1 Sambon Foreloader, 3 Renault vans, 1 Leyland cattle lorry, 2 ten ton trailers, 3 six and a half ton trailers, cultivation equipment, ploughs, harrows and the irrigation plant. He nursed the 2 Class 106 combines through each harvest, constantly being called out to fix them. Then the forestry department had 2 Ford tractors, 1 Ford 5000 tractor with a crane and trailer, a Bedford timber lorry, a sawbench, a landrover, chainsaws and other equipment, and a Ford Major tractor with winch. These machines were all cared for by Heinz. He serviced all the garden machinery including a Ferguson and a Ford tractor, a dumper truck, and various lawnmowers. Finally, he looked after not only the family cars, but also the agent's car, the Clerk of the Works lorry, and the keeper's Landrover. He worked mostly on his own.

apparently the brakes failed. After testing the brakes no fault was found. This was not the end of it. This particular driver was very vocal and insisted the brakes had failed, so the management gave instructions to have the whole braking system overhauled. It was a totally useless exercise, as nothing was wrong with it, and it was a great waste of money. After that, I decided to weld the pedals together, and then the fun started. The same driver wrote to the Ford Motor Company and complained that the brake pedals on his tractor had been welded together. I never discovered the company's reaction. I am sure they were falling over the place laughing, but I suppose the driver scored points in the end as the weld was cut. The third incident which I

The Trees of Hatfield Park

RIK PAKENHAM

Rik Pakenham is a forester who leads Chiltern Forestry a management and consultancy company based near Oxford. The core business is woodland and tree management advice for private landowners in southern England. He also works on European research projects and forestry investment in the Baltics. He has been advising at Hatfield since 2006.

HATFIELD is unusual in that the Estate offers a remarkably diverse collection of trees, from those offering shade to the more delicate shrubs and small trees in the Shrubbery to the blocks of conifer planted after the Second World War. There are ancient oaks, formal avenues, and sturdy stockproof hedgerows of thorn and hazel. Some fragments of the woodland may well retain links with the original 'wildwood' that grew up after the last Ice Age.

VETERANS

The Park has a fine collection of veteran trees, adding greatly to its character. Such is their importance that they are in the process of being recorded and mapped using GPS to plot their positions. A management plan has been compiled. Old maps and archive records were consulted to build up a picture of their history.

A veteran tree is defined as 'a tree that is of interest biologically, culturally or aesthetically because of its age, size or condition'. Historically they link us with our past and illustrate how we used to live and interact with our environment. They are also rare, and Britain contains 75% of all the veteran trees in Europe. Ecologically, ancient trees are an important habitat, particularly for

OPPOSITE The Elephant Oak is probably between 1,000 to 1,200 years old. It is named because it looks like an elephant, and gives its name to the whole area known as Elephant Dell where many other veteran oaks are situated.

invertebrates that live on dead and decaying wood, but they also provide a range of habitats for mammals, birds, bats, lichens and mosses.

The following list gives some idea of the wide range of species in Hatfield Park: Elephant Dell (predominantly oak in wood pasture), Coombe Wood (hornbeam, lane edge trees), South Avenue (a lime avenue), Showground (oak park boundary trees from Little Park, the original park around the Old Palace), Conduit Wood (ash and hawthorn ancient hedgerow), Guides Road (oak and hornbeam road edge trees), Park Dairy (oak scattered parkland trees).

Many of the trees in the park are pollards, which mean they have been managed by regularly cutting the crown which then regrows ready to be cut again ten to thirty years later depending on the species. The trees are pollarded at about 2 metres from the ground, a height that grazing animals such as deer and cattle cannot reach. They were traditionally cut when in leaf, thus producing fodder for livestock as well as timber for firewood, charcoal and construction.

This type of management system is called wood pasture, which means that the trees are widely spaced in a grassland setting. The regular cutting prolongs the life of a tree to such an extent that the oldest tree in the Park is an oak that has been aged at 1200 years, approximately 800 years older than the House itself.

New trees are being planted, some of which will eventually be pollarded to retain and enhance these land-

scape features and habitats. Seed is collected and grown on to retain the same genetic base, which is obviously well adapted to the soils within the Park.

There are also many maiden trees (not pollarded) scattered throughout the Park. These would have been planted to improve the look of the landscape, to provide shade for livestock, timber for building work, and, in the case of oak and beech, acorns and beech nuts to be foraged by pigs.

AVENUES

The formal planting of avenues in England started in the early seventeeth century, but came to us via a long line of influences, including Italian Renaissance gardens and the Baroque garden style, typified by Versailles in France, where the allee, a straight path lined with trees or shrubs, was used to great effect.

Such was their popularity that today there are 3.5 miles of avenues in the Park at Hatfield. The map of 1610 shows that the South, North, Queen Elizabeth and Castle Avenues, as well as part of the West Avenue, were planted at the same time as the House was being built. None of the original trees remain from this date, and the oldest are the limes at the end of the South Avenue which were planted in about 1700.

The principal species is lime. However the North Avenue has an inner row of beech, and the East Avenue consists of evergreen oak. They vary in ages from 15 to 300 + years old. The majority are currently planted as double rows, albeit of different ages. However all but

A veteran hornbeam pollard in Coombe Wood, probably 600 years old.

the South Avenue is shown as single rows on the 1786 map, but by 1870 many were shown as double.

There are two native species of lime, Small-leaved Lime (*Tilia cordata*) and Broad-leaved Lime (*Tilia platyphyllos*). These produce a natural hybrid, albeit relatively rarely in England, called Common Lime (*Tilia europaea*). This offspring has hybrid vigour and is easy to clone, traits that the Dutch nurserymen exploited in the seventeenth century, leading to many of our avenues being planted with Common Lime imported from Holland.

Research carried out by Dr. C.D. Pigott of Cambridge University Botanic Gardens, some of which was done at Hatfield House, shows that most avenues planted between 1600 and 1750 were predominantly two clones of Common Lime – Clonal Group A T. *x europaea* 'pallida' and Clonal Group B, which Dr Pigott proposed be named T *x europaea* 'Hatfield Tall'. Most of the

Parſonage

North Mims

TOTTERIDGE PARK

ABOVE *Queen Elizabeth Avenue looking east, thought to have been planted in the mid nineteenth century with Common Lime.*

OPPOSITE *Map dated 1786 shows the house, park and surrounding fields. Many of the features are as illustrated on the earlier 1610 map compiled as the house was being built. The avenues and woods are still present today.*

characteristics are identical to Dutch clones. Both of these are planted at Hatfield and are visually quite different.

A long-term rejuvenation plan is being implemented to make sure this historical feature is retained. Due to their age, many trees are potentially dangerous in areas of high public access, especially once dieback and rot set in. Attempts to help retain these trees for as long as possible will be implemented, but at the same time new trees are being planted which will eventually replace them.

WOODLANDS

It is difficult to decide where the Park starts and finishes with regards to the woodland blocks. With most of the north, west and south sides within a Park fence this leaves the eastern edge open for discussion. However, if the boundary is from Hillend via West End Lane and

Green Street, the total area is approximately 367 hectares (907 acres).

Millwards and part of Deave Wood are scheduled as plantations on ancient woodland sites (PAWS). This means that they have been woodland since at least 1600, with probable links way back to the original 'wildwood' that developed after the last Ice Age 12,000 years ago. The remaining area has no designation so would originally have been fields and wood pasture. However, contemporary plans from 1603 show Combes Wood and Conduit Grove, and the 1768 estate maps show Coombe Wood, part of Conduit, the Bushes and the centre of Brickkiln as woodland. So these may also be ancient woodlands that have been missed off the register.

Ninety percent of this area has been felled and/or re-planted since the Second World War, approximately 65% with conifers and 35% with broadleaved trees,

Timber forwarder working in Millwards Park. This machine is used to extract timber that has been felled and cross cut into various different lengths depending on the specification for the end use. On this load are Scots Pine Shavers which are chipped, dust extracted and sold for horse bedding. Note hydraulic grab used to pick up the timber.

usually in mixes. Fortunately many old and veteran trees were spared, and survive today throughout most of the plantations.

The high percentage of conifer is the result of a government policy to replant with fast growing conifers to replenish a timber reserve that was much depleted after two world wars. Only 4% of the country was woodland in the late 1940s.

That policy has largely been reversed, and the trend is a gradual increase in the number of broadleaved trees native to Hertfordshire, while avoiding clear felling of large areas – thus helping to make the woodlands at Hatfield as diverse as possible.

The primary management objectives now include enhancing biodiversity, retaining the historic landscape, timber production, preserving historic and archaeological features, whilst at the same time improving and securing the long term future of all types of trees for the benefit of the Cecil family, and the many thousands of visitors who annually enjoy the Park.

Another area in the park of a group of veteran oak pollards, now situated in a wild daffodil meadow.

The Future – Going Local

NED CRANBORNE

HATFIELD HOUSE and the Old Palace were built for purposes which can now only be regarded as anachronistic. So what should happen to a latter day prodigy house fit to host a king and impress on others the status of the owner?

A second political flowering, in the late nineteenth century, meant that conversations in the house on national and international affairs were once more conducted by those in a position to influence or make decisions. But in the highly unlikely event of future Cecils reaching such political heights as the 3rd Marquess of Salisbury or his ancestor, the 1st Earl, the house could not in today's or tomorrow's world serve its original purpose. It would also fail to provide a roof over the heads of a modern day 'Hotel Cecil' – as relations of the Prime Minister Salisbury were sometimes rather disparagingly called. What extended family would now be willing to spend all their time together, and what country would allow so many of their senior politicians to share the same blood?

Yet the vitality of all the people connected to the place means Hatfield cannot spend much time reflecting on the past. Even the archive department demonstrates this with its involvement in a digitisation process. I believe it is on a local rather than a national stage that Hatfield will find its place in the third millennium. Of course there have always been connections between Hatfield and the county but now because the rural Hertfordshire of Elizabeth Bennett has gone forever, there is a far more diverse and complex future for the county and therefore, by association, the House and Estate.

So, I am charged with the tricky task of writing about what might happen in the future. An estate is amongst other things a collection of small businesses and interests bundled together. Originally this made sense, both as the economic and administrative unit of a manor and as a useful means by which feudal overlords might exercise control. In a world where the apparent economic imperative has led to ever greater specialisations and increases in scale, I would regard this old-fashioned diversity as a strength. When one area, say agriculture, is weak then another area such as visitor attractions might be strong and this has meant that, so far, the place has remained largely intact. This also gives an opportunity to participate in and learn about local enterprise, be it social or economic, frequently in areas where the Estate already has exposure and occasionally in new spheres.

Development within the county is a particularly contentious example where the Estate has recently tried to engage in a positive manner in conjunction with local partners. Although Hertfordshire is blessed with many fine buildings, and towns such as Welwyn and Letchworth are models of imaginative and creative town planning, more recent efforts have been pitiful. Yet because Hatfield has on its very doorstep the Watford-based Building Research Establishment, sympathetic local officials and councillors and, in the local university, a rigorous academic interest in how people engage in future development in this county, Hertfordshire should be, and will be, at the front of innovative and thoughtful development.

It is possible to be innovative in more conventional Estate businesses. Rik Packenham, who advises on forestry matters, has taken the Estate down a less intrusive European style of management that avoids the clear felling of trees and allows their natural regeneration to replace those which have been extracted. This has mirrored actions taken at Cranborne in Dorset, where I live, and is one example of many where the cross-fertilization of ideas between the two Estates has yielded benefits. This development in woodland management is a radical change from the past, although it has been common in Europe and on one or two places in England, such as Longleat, for some time.

Regarding Estate social endeavours, educational efforts, made under the title of 'Living History', which have been expanded under the guidance of Sue Jessup, further extend interaction with the locality. No doubt this benefits the children who visit, but it also reminds us why we are all here.

There is one thing that keeps this whole varied enterprise together – and in surprisingly coherent form. I have on occasion heard my father affectionately describe it as a white elephant: 'it' is of course the House. The House conjures up in my mind not just a building but also all the people in it, now and from the past.

These two last are often difficult to consolidate in one's mind. My great-great uncle David put it as succinctly as ever in his book *The Cecils of Hatfield House*: 'My parents and even my grandparents are part of my own experience; they have contributed, I realize, to my own identity. But when I peer back through the mists of the past in search of more distant ancestors, I find myself confronting the faces of those who, though they may bear the same name as mine, are in fact strangers, with whom I feel no sense of personal connection, and who, however much I study their stories, will always remain for me figures in a history book.'

Perhaps the Estate's historical support for innovation will be a guide for the direction taken in the future. This past enthusiasm for the new included radical crop-rotating ideas of the 1st Marchioness. Support was shown for the arrival of the train by the 3rd Marquess who, with his strong scientific bent, also developed the early hydroelectric power generated lights which meant that Hatfield vied with Craigside in Northumberland to be one of the first houses to install electricity. The wooden trunking that can still be seen around the house is a relic from that pre-health and safety age. Even the tank, the prototype of that which first saw action at the Somme, sat rusting until quite recently as a reminder of its first trials that took place in the Park. Inspiration can also be taken from local efforts as diverse as building the Mosquito at the old de Havilland aerodrome site or the cultural influence of that Yorkshireman Henry Moore, who lived nearby. It all adds to the lustre of what is Hertfordshire, and Hatfield is very much part of Hertfordshire.

Like Mervyn Peake's Gormenghast, Hatfield could so easily become stagnant and introspective, yet because of the people who are involved it has become increasingly engaged. The future should build on this and I hope the Estate will become involved in some of Hertfordshire's future successes. The Hatfield Estate will of course be influenced by the ethos, tone, attitude and even prejudices of the past. Perhaps that is the best thing that it can bring to the table. By engaging with the wider world, paying far more than lip service to the past but also participating in the future, we will ensure the place thrives rather than petrifies.

Hatfield House from the south.

Acknowledgements

To THANK the many people who have made the publication of this book possible is no small task. Naturally I start with my contributors who heroically wrote most of the chapters in this book and without whom this project would never have happened. They were unbelievably generous with both their time and their knowledge. I would also like to thank Frank Lodge and Heinz Kuntze for their rural memories, as well as the Hatfield Guides, Mrs Dorothy Craggs, Mrs Jam Cartwright and Mrs Pamela Brown for their vignettes about showing the house, and Kevin Dean for his recipes.

I owe a huge debt of gratitude to David Burnett of the Dovecote Press who worked tirelessly on the draft chapters, encouraging me and following up meticulously every inconsistency and caption. My thanks also go to his assistant Elizabeth Dean who worked so hard co-ordinating the chapters. I am indebted to Humphrey Stone who designed not only the book but also had the idea of using the earliest painting of Hatfield House for the jacket. I am grateful to my daughter Georgiana Campbell for her subediting and whose advice has been invaluable. Thank you to Douglas Slater and Bruce Anderson for proofreading. Thank you, too, to Robin Harcourt Williams, our archivist at Hatfield, who made sure there were no mistakes of a historical nature, proofread, and applied his knowledge and experience of both the estate and the archives.

I am also indebted to Sir Kenneth Rose for allowing me to quote extensively from his book *The Later Cecils* and to Mr Nick Robinson of Constable Robinson for permission to include passages from Lord David Cecil's book *The Cecils of Hatfield House*.

I owe a debt of gratitude to the many photographers and it is difficult to name each of them individually. The professionals, Antoinette Eugster, Phil Starling and Rob Burton, generously allowed me to use their photographs. I am indebted to Nigel Woodhouse and Michael Perry for their photographs, together with many others who have been equally generous. Elaine Gunn and Vicky Perry masterminded this exercise, using their technical skills, and without them I should have been helpless. Thank you to Cherise Fairman, Julie Loughlin, Alison MacDonald, Alastair Gunn, Ann Maidment and Lindsay Warwick Gee for their help in drawing together the strings of what has proven to be a complicated operation. Lastly I would like to thank my husband Robert Salisbury, who encouraged and supported me throughout, and who strived to improve my use of English and who dissuaded me from using the passive tense.

Index